Jimmy Simpson

Legend of
the Rockies

James Simpson Jr.

Mary Simpson Hallock

E.J. HART

Jimmy Simpson

Legend of the Rockies

Altitude Publishing
Banff Alberta Canada

For Pat ... finally.

Canadian Cataloguing in Publication Data
Hart, E. J. (Edward John), 1946–
Jimmy Simpson, Legend of the Rockies
ISBN 0-919381-53-7 hardcover
ISBN 0-919381-09-X paperback
1. Simpson, Jimmy. 2. Mountaineering guides (Persons) –
Rocky Mountains, Canadian (B.C. and Alta.) – Biography.*
3. Mountaineering – Rocky Mountains, Canadian (B.C. and Alta.).*
4. Rocky Mountains, Canadian (B.C. and Alta.) – Description and travel.* I. Title.
FC218.S54H37 1990   917.11'0092   C90-091609-5
F1090.H37 1990

This book was written and published with the assistance of
the Alberta Foundation for the Literary Arts and Alberta Culture
and Multiculturalism, Film and Literary Arts Branch

Design: Robert MacDonald, MediaClones Inc.,
Toronto, Vancouver, and Banff Canada

Front cover photograph hand coloured by Carole Harmon

Altitude Publishing
Post Office Box 490
Banff Alberta Canada T0L 0C0

Printed in Canada

TABLE OF CONTENTS

ACKNOWLEDGEMENTS

As is the case with most works of this type, it would not have been possible without the support and cooperation of several groups and individuals, and I would like to take this opportunity to acknowledge this fact.

First of all, I would like to thank the Alberta Foundation for the Literary Arts who provided a grant that allowed for the time and resources to make the research and writing of this manuscript possible. We writers in Alberta are particularly fortunate to have the support of such an organization, the envy of many of our writing brethren across the country.

Secondly, I would like to thank my employer, the Whyte Museum of the Canadian Rockies, for their understanding and flexibility in scheduling during the period when much of the intense writing was being done. As usual, they have graciously supported my work as an extension of the mandate they foster — the collection and dissemination of the history and culture of the Canadian Rockies.

Thirdly, I would like to thank the numerous archivists and librarians who helped to ferret out much of the information that went into this work — particularly those at the Whyte Museum and the National Archives of Canada.

Fourthly, my appreciation to all of those who provided personal reminiscences and information in response to my constant queries. Although they are numerous, I would like to say a special thanks to Mary Hallock and Jimmy Simpson jr. who asked me to undertake the work and never failed to provide a story or a missing link when it was needed.

Finally, I would like to thank my wife Pat for assisting with the research when other duties called me away and for her unfailing support and understanding during the long evenings and weekends when most of the work had to be done.

E.J. Hart
Banff
March 1, 1991

INTRODUCTION

Nashan-esen paused to rest from the exertion of breaking trail on his journey up the North Saskatchewan River. It was one of the last days of 1903 and as he halted he recalled the "Christmas dinner etc." he had just survived at Tom Wilson's cabin on the Kootenay Plains. Wild sheep had stood in for the Christmas turkey and rum had provided the trimmings, leaving both men somewhat ornery. Despite the fact that he had snowshoed for five days and covered 75 miles from his trapline to accept the invitation, the conversation had quickly dwindled, and Wilson's "When the Hell are you going back?" had sent him on his way. For several hours he had been snowshoeing with the speed that had earned him the name Nashan-esen, meaning "wolverine-go-quick," from the Stoney Indians, and the rest he took was short for he was anxious to get back to his headquarters deep in the Canadian Rockies, between Bow Pass and Jonas Creek. As he resumed the trek, his mind dancing with thoughts of the prime marten pelts that should await him in his traps, he followed the path of least resistance on some lightly snow-covered ice formed by the river choking up above a waterfall. It was a mistake — one that a lone wilderness traveller could ill-afford to make.

The ice collapsed with a crash into the cavity formed where the water level had subsided when the obstruction cleared. But on this day Nashan-esen's luck was good. As his snowshoes disappeared into the freezing depths and his mackinaw pants slid on sloping ice, his fingers fell into a crack and, since he was carrying only a light pack and an axe, he had little extra weight to drag him down. Instinctively, a number of thoughts pushed into a mind attuned to the perils of the wilderness: "You must keep the axe. To lose a snowshoe is equally fatal even though the current is sucking at them and nearly pulling you under. There is always the desire to kick them loose. But you hesitate! You must pull yourself to safety, slowly, carefully, so as not by too much sudden action tread loose your frail hold, and behind you, under you, is blue black water that is not hesitating on its way to the Atlantic." The cool head prevailed and inch by excruciating inch he pulled his wiry frame onto firmer ice and then quickly scrambled to the bush flanking the river.

Already his mackinaw pants were stiffening, but he realized that before anything could be taken off, the recently saved tool of survival, the axe, had to be used to cut down a dry pine and split it to make a fire; otherwise, "it is going to be slow music for you some time next summer if what is left of you happens to be found." Then, before his fingers were completely numbed, he fumbled a match out of the waterproof container in his pack, struck it, and, shivering almost uncontrollably, held it patiently to the wood until the frost came out and the flame sputtered to life.

After drying out completely before the warming fire and thanking his lucky stars he would probably live to see his twenty-seventh birthday, Nashan-esen slipped his shoepacks into the thongs mounted to the bootboards of his snowshoes and set off once more. But the lessons of this trip, one that an older and wiser Jimmy Simpson would recall "furnished the closest misses to the final exit I have ever made," were not yet over. The following day, as he was travelling in a dry creek bed under steep cut-banks, his wilderness education continued. The day was warm enough to leave his shirt and undershirt wide open and he was moving fast, bent on making a favourite camping spot and gathering plenty of wood before nightfall. Suddenly, he heard a soughing noise and glanced up just in time to see a snow slide come pouring down on him. The deep breaths of exertion from his fast pace immediately filled his lungs with suffocating powder but, at the last moment, seeing his dog plunge its nose into the settled snow, he got his woollen mitts to his mouth to prevent himself from choking. Luckily, he remained near the surface of the jumbled mass, but as his shirt was stuffed with packed snow it was an exhausting struggle to free himself quickly from the deadly white prison. By the time he succeeded and was once more able to set off for camp, he was soaking wet and chilled to the bone.

The camp was not far off and, having been used before Christmas, it housed a bit of wood ready for a fire. Soon the warming flames had taken the chill out of the weary traveller's bones, but he was too exhausted even to eat before rolling into his sleeping robe and falling into a deep slumber. Waking early with a ravenous appetite, he began to cook a meal — "fry bacon and imagine the eggs." When the bacon was nearly cooked he noticed that some frost had fallen into it and, looking up, saw a

Whiskey Jack on the branch of a tree above him. A few choice expletives cast in its direction soon had the offender on its way, and the cook bent over the frying pan to give the bacon one last turn. Much to his amazement, more frost dropped into the pan. Looking up at the tree again, he thought to himself that it was strange frost would be falling from a branch that had had a fire burning under it all night. Then slowly the realization of what was happening dawned on him. The top of a vial of strychnine he carried in his shirt pocket for use on the trapline had worked loose, and the supposed "frost" was actually enough deadly poison to kill any wolverine! The pan was quickly cleaned with a few handfuls of snow and Nashan-esen was soon musing over the trip's lessons while he wolfed down a fresh rasher of bacon.

Such was life in the wilderness of the Canadian Rockies for Jimmy Simpson, taken in stride with the lessons learned and never forgotten. When well into his nineties, Jimmy was asked by a friend what his years of experience had taught him. He unhesitatingly replied that his life could be summed up by the axiom, "If you listen the wilderness teaches you. If you don't, it can kill you." Three-quarters-of-a-century of life in the Rockies had been akin to an education for Jimmy, the passing grade being survival in the face of the hazards this rugged and beautiful landscape held.

And what a life it was — a storybook-style epic of a man, not pitted against nature but rather working with it to achieve an almost larger-than-life reputation. This book is an attempt to tell some of that story — to present the life of Justin James McCarthy Simpson with its ups and downs, its triumphs and tragedies, its humour and tall-tales and its messages for future generations of mountain wilderness lovers. Unfortunately, Jimmy never wrote his own biography, despite the attempts of many to get him to do so. But because he became a legend in his own time, Jimmy often reminisced or wrote about his experiences in letters and stories. Wherever possible I have used his own words, delivered in his own inimitable fashion, to tell the tale.

Here then is the story of Nashan-esen, legend of the Rockies, the last and greatest of the Canadian mountain men.

CHAPTER ONE

Footloose in America

As Jimmy told it, it all started when he disgraced the family in church.

Justin James McCarthy Simpson had been born on August 8, 1877 in England at Stamford, Lincolnshire. Stamford was a market town that had a long history dating to pre-Roman Conquest times, as it was here that early travellers had found an easy crossing of the Welland River. His father, Justin Simpson, had a keen interest in those ancient times. A scholarly man, he wrote several books on the history and genealogy of the area, including *A List of the Monumental Brasses of England* in 1857 and *Obituary and Records for the Counties of Lincoln, Rutland and Northampton* in 1861. The "McCarthy" in his son's name came from a friend who had written a history of Stamford at the time of King Charles. The Simpson family actually had a coat-of-arms bestowed on it by the same King Charles, but Jimmy never showed it around once he got to Canada, believing "most people would think it was an advertisement of Beecham's Pills."

Jimmy's mother, Elizabeth Riley, was of Irish descent and bore two other children, Elizabeth, her eldest child, and Nancy, who died at a young age. Although his father's scholarly background provides a clue to Jimmy's intelligent and inquisitive nature, neither of his parents appear to have had much of an influence on him. His mother died when he was a youngster and his upbringing was left largely in the hands of his Aunt Susan. She did the best she could with the rambunctious lad, trying to make sure that he attended classes regularly at Stamford Grammar School. But Jimmy was a rascally youth, constantly disappointing his aunt and father and taxing their rather dour senses of propriety. One of his favourite pastimes was poaching the abundant pheasants and rabbits on the nearby Marquis of Exeter's estate, although this had its drawbacks because "the gamekeepers had size 17 shoes and put them behind me until I was nearly humpbacked." In February, 1896, when he was eighteen years old, Jimmy's father died, and he came under the guardianship of his Uncle Henry. Henry Simpson, a seedsman and brewer, was a man of substance in Stamford, having served a period as mayor. He was therefore able to provide his nephew with the best opportunities for advancement available. He tried Jimmy at several trades, first as a printer's devil, "and devil was the right word because I broke up the front sheet of a paper as it was just going to press." This was followed by a stint as a newspaper distributor, a career that ended abruptly when he threw the papers in the river in favour of going off poaching on the Marquis' lands. The final straw came at church in March, 1896 and, according to Jimmy, it happened in this way:

The family pew was up close to the altar and the lesser fry of the congregation were in the stalls. That made the family somewhat hoity-toity. The little vicar got playing around with the lady organist, so he was asked to send in his resignation, which he did and stated that he would preach his last sermon the following Sunday. I had to be there, but instead of pushing to the far end of the pew, somehow I was the last in which made me first to get out. He preached a good sermon, asked the congregation for no condolences, but they could watch him leave them perhaps forever. As he passed down the aisle I let off a big laugh and pointed to his back. On his coat-tails there was pinned a bunch of mistletoe and kissing under the mistletoe was in vogue in Queen Victoria's time.

Convinced that Jimmy was born to be hanged, his uncle threatened to send him off to Australia, a part of the colonies usually reserved for those with criminal proclivities. But Jimmy had heard something of another colony, Canada, where his father had gone in 1860 to serve as a guard for the Prince of Wales, later King Edward VII, during a royal visit. Relenting one last time, Henry Simpson conversed with his contacts and discovered the possibility of a farming career near Winnipeg for his wayward nephew.

So it was that late in March, 1896 the Simpson family gathered at the

Liverpool docks to see Jimmy off to the New World. Inside his new suit of clothes were sewn enough sovereigns to see to his immediate needs, including the necessary farm lands. The girl with whom he had been keeping company was there with the family to see him off, apparently believing it would not be too long before he would return. He himself thought he would be back in about six months and when he bid the family farewell and said he would see them in that length of time "there wasn't a cheer in the bunch." As for the young lady, Jimmy later mused, "If she's waiting there to welcome me back, she's wet clean through," for he was never again to visit the land of his birth.

The year that Jimmy arrived in Canada, 1896, is generally regarded as a key date in the history of the west. It was the time that the Laurier government, following the lead of its vociferous Minister of the Interior Clifford Sifton, unleashed their efforts to attract immigrants from around the world to settle the unpopulated agricultural Eden of western Canada. Perhaps Jimmy had been partially attracted by the strains of early agricultural advertising campaigns, but if so it was not to take firm root. After arriving in Winnipeg, Jimmy travelled south to La Riviére to view the farm his uncle had arranged for him to buy. One look at the sod shack and rather bleak surroundings convinced him that farming was not for him, so within two days he was back in Winnipeg firmly ensconced in a boarding house on Arthur Street, and he quickly "cheered up Winnipeg with some good fresh English money."

But if he did not fit into the agricultural mould of so many other immigrants arriving at the time, Jimmy was certainly their equal in his enthusiasm for the country. Little is known of his background and life in England because he would rarely talk about it after his arrival in Canada. For his remaining eighty years, there was only one thing that mattered — the country he had chosen and its unlimited opportunities for those who wished to pursue them. Canada, the west, and particularly the mountains were everything of importance, while England and his past were of small consequence. When anyone took the trouble to question him on this, he pointed out that in England "everything was keep off this or keep out of that." Unlike his uncle, he believed that he was "born for the outdoors" and in Canada he could go where he wished and do what he pleased.

The boarders on Arthur Street were the main benefactors of Jimmy's remittance, and soon it was drunk up. Having listened in awe to the stories of the west told by the old timers in Winnipeg, he pawned his gold watch and chain and bought passage for Calgary on a cattle train. On arriving there, he ran into some of the boys from Arthur Street, who were heading further west to go to work for the Canadian Pacific Railway on a wash-out near Golden. They convinced him to come along, but as he was now without means a little subterfuge was called for. Before long he found himself a stowaway on a westbound CPR train, neatly closed into an upper bunk by his friends. It proved too comfortable a hiding place and before long his snoring attracted the attention of a passing conductor. The bunk was pulled down, the stowaway captured and summarily booted off the train at the next stop.

As fate would have it, on being ejected from the train Jimmy found himself in the midst of a wonderland unlike anything he had ever dreamed of. The station was Castle Mountain and as he walked along the line to the next station at Laggan, near Lake Louise, he marvelled at the peaks clad with fresh spring snow towering into the cerulean sky. It was an impressive sight, and one that obviously had a great effect on the young Englishman. However, there was a more pressing concern than the scenery — how to keep body and soul together. The CPR was really the only game in town and soon he found himself in their employ using "tools I had never seen before, i.e. pick and shovel." To his amazement he found he liked the work, probably because it was something new and it took place in such magnificent surroundings.

During this period, Jimmy befriended an old trapper by the name of Smith who lived at Lake Louise, and this veteran of the mountains took him along on a few of his outings, providing some basic knowledge that would eventually become very useful. But another acquaintance made at this time was to prove even more influential on the future course of Jimmy's life.

One October evening he heard a tinkling sound opposite the Laggan railway station and wandered over to investigate. He found three horses with bells on their necks standing near a tent. Peering inside, he was invited to enter by the lone occupant:

I saw a man lying on his blankets, his head on his open palms, a rifle on his left side and a wicked looking revolver near his right hand. Very black as to the hair with deep sunken blue eyes he pictured my ideal man that I had dreamed of as a kid and here he was in the flesh. He was just in from a prospecting trip and the cuts on his chin showed he had shaved with his hunting knife, and not too well at that, but it all fitted the man himself. A look around the tent showed saddles and cooking pots and a heap of copper samples that to me resembled gold or some precious metal and I was thrilled.

Fate had brought him into the presence of E. W. "Bill" Peyto, a man who Jimmy later described as his "teenage hero" and one who "I was determined to emulate or die in the attempt." Peyto was a fellow Englishman, a native of Welling, Kent, who had arrived in Canada a decade earlier and had travelled it end-to-end before adopting the life of a trapper and prospector in the Rockies. A few years before meeting Jimmy, he had also begun to spend part of his time as a guide for the numerous tourists beginning to visit the mountains, although the major part of his career as the area's most colourful early guide and outfitter was still ahead of him. In any event, Jimmy was face-to-face with his first mountain man, "straight as an arrow and thoroughly well groomed although roughly clothed." In response to Peyto's gruff question of "Whose kid are you?," he explained that he was just out from England, and that seemed to break the ice — the evening was spent with Bill recounting some of his adventures and misadventures. But when Jimmy returned for another visit just after breakfast the next morning he found his new acquaintance had already pulled out for Banff. Nevertheless, the seed was sown.

Perhaps the brief encounter with Peyto and the tales of his travels had stirred the spirit of wanderlust in Jimmy's soul, or perhaps he had already intended to see something of North America. Whichever it was, when November arrived and he was laid off his labouring job, he decided to head out. Reflecting later on his sojourn at Lake Louise and the effect it had on him he said, "Mixing with men who had built the Canadian Pacific and some who had crossed the prairie in a covered wagon was the medicine I needed." Feeling much more like a man who had proven himself with the best, he set off for the coast.

Fortunately the trip to Vancouver cost him very little, because he knew most of the conductors along the line and they passed him from one to another. Then after a short stay in the coastal city, he beat it south for the legendary San Francisco "to see the sights on 50 dollars." Jimmy recalled that it was "wide open as a church door but not for the same reasons," and he soon fell in with some of the rough-and-tumble characters who had given the city its reputation. Quickly using up his scant funds, he found himself bound for Los Angeles underneath the wheel carriage of a Southern Pacific Railway train. At Fresno he was discovered by a railway policeman, who ordered him out of his hiding place. He made a run for it but promptly dodged down an alley into a brick wall and was easily collared. However, he found that his arrest wasn't such bad luck after all. The magistrate sentenced him to five days in the hobo gaol, a heated building where he could rest up and get three meals a day, and during his incarceration he played cards with the older inmates most of the time and "learned the rudiments of the great American game of draw poker," a skill he would use many times in his life thereafter.

When he was released, Jimmy was given twenty minutes to get out of town and "I beat the time by ten on a freight" headed for Oceana. There he worked in a coal mine for a short time before hearing of the possibility of employment in an asphalt mine not far from Santa Barbara. To get to the mine he had to walk 60 miles over Gaviota Pass and he arrived on a Sunday morning nearly starved: "I asked the Chinese cook for something to eat and without a smile he asked me if I liked fish. About then I could have eaten a shark, fins, tail and head, and I said so. With the same countenance he replied, 'Come alound Fliday'."

Jimmy couldn't wait until Friday, so he again found a convenient freight train and hopped a ride into Santa Barbara. Upon arriving, he fell in with a band of a thousand hobos under the leadership of a self-styled General Kelly. These were depression times in California and the hobos were intent on marching to Washington to place their grievances before the president. Although he never fully understood the nature of their complaints, Jimmy decided to go along for the experience. The decision led to an acquaintance with Jack London, "a tough, wharf-bred rat who later became California's greatest author." He and London were assigned to the advance group of the hobo caravan, responsible for going ahead into the towns to warn the people the gang was coming and advise them that they better have food ready if they didn't want their town wrecked. Jimmy soon decided that this was getting a bit too strong for his taste, and he left the army at a place named Grants, west of Albuquerque, New Mexico, where he found a job on the Santa Fe Railway loading steel rails. Because of his experience as a labourer on the CPR, he took easily to the work on the Santa Fe. Before too long, he noticed the system the men were using to load the rails was inefficient and showed them how it was done in Canada. This impressed the foreman and he asked Jimmy to stay on and take over a crew of Mexicans to boss. Responsibility was the last thing he wanted, so he headed back for San Francisco. There he almost fell prey to the clutches of a dancehall girl, but was saved by the police:

I stayed off in San Francisco and got acquainted with a girl who was selling drinks in a dancehall on commission, and she wanted me to go over to Bakersfield with her; but during the conversation I found she had two children, so I went outside to think it over. It was on Kerney Street. When I got outside I was grabbed by a big athletic policeman who pushed me ahead and put number sixteen shoes behind me right down to Market Street, and that was three blocks. I was hump backed for a week, and I never went back.

This time the freight he caught was heading north, and he soon found himself in Oregon working for a lumber company. Three months of hard labour replenished his grubstake, but he got paid off in $5 gold pieces and they had soon slipped through his fingers, leading to a "religious experience:"

I went and got gloriously tight in a little place called Cottage Grove and then beat my way up to Salem, dead broke again and nearly asleep standing up as I hadn't had a good bed for weeks. I saw an open building with a lot of people inside & I thought it was a meeting of some kind. I thought if I can get in there I can find an empty chair and sit down and go to sleep. But it was a meeting of holy rollers, a peculiar religious sect, and the head of it was exhorting his people to 'Get down on your knees, get down on your knees, we're going to have a Jesus hunt.' Somebody put out the lights, and it was as dark as the inside of a cow, and I heard them scrambling all over the floor. Pretty soon a woman screamed and a man yelled 'I've got him, I've got him by the beard.' He'd been at those meetings before and knew the ropes.

Leaving Salem, Jimmy made his way north to Vancouver, and then east on the CPR in search of work with his old employer. At Illecillewaet in Rogers Pass he got a job taking out the original twin wooden trestle bridges, which were being replaced by steel ones. The hours of work were long but so were the summer days and he was afforded the opportunity to acquaint himself with a mountain area that was quite different from the one he had experienced around Lake Louise. Here the valleys were narrower and more precipitous, the forests thicker and carpeted with rank undergrowth from the heavy precipitation, and the woods were full of grizzly bears. Although not immediately useful, the information was stored away in his memory to be used later.

He also remembered this summer for another reason — it gave him the opportunity to listen to the best tenor singer he ever heard. An aficinado of the great voices of his day, he was later to hear such stars as Scotti, Caruso and Geraldine Ferrar in New York, but Jimmy reported that a little barrel-chested Italian working with him outdid them all. One day during one of their infrequent rest breaks, the man, who was living in the bunk car next to Jimmy, was washing some of his clothes and started singing "O Sole Mio." Jimmy went over to listen and then poked his head out of the car to see 150 men who had put down their tools and gathered around to hear this beautiful voice, as if drawn by a magnet. Jimmy asked, "Pedro, what in the name of Mica with a voice like that are you doing working for a bunch like this? Why don't you sing for a living?" "Me sing for a living," the Italian replied, "and lose a dollar-and-a-half a day!"

Having found his first trip to California an exciting and seductive experience, Jimmy decided to head south again in the fall of 1897. Most of that winter was spent in San Pedro with the usual results; early the following spring he found himself in need of a grubstake. This time he decided to try something entirely new — the sea.

Numerous coasting vessels embarked from San Francisco Bay and he had no difficulty finding a position. On March 1, 1898 he signed on as a seaman on the sailing schooner *Mermaid*, of Victoria, B.C. registry, and spent the next two months seal hunting off the coasts of California and Vancouver Island. Because the ship had a Siwash Indian crew, Jimmy was afforded his first opportunity to learn something of North American natives, a people with which he was to become very familiar. In later years, he remembered an incident that gave him insight into how Indians, and others attuned to nature, could sense and avoid danger:

It is not realised by the mass of people that Indians and out-of-doors men have & our forefathers had intuitions in hunting or of dangers ahead that ordinary individuals do not have & I remember that once off the mouth of the Columbia River we would have been cut in half by a coast steamer riding without lights had it not been for one of the Indians coming up on deck in the night, lighting a piece of waste & throwing it up in the air. The steamer veered off & narrowly missed us. I asked the Indian what made him come up on deck, out of bed & do it but he just answered 'Me feel em.'

Jimmy went on to say that the plains Indian had similar intuitions while hunting, and knew where game would be, and that "in my more energetic days I had it too."

Jimmy survived the sealing voyage intact and took his discharge in Victoria when the ship docked on May 7, 1898, receiving a rating of "very good" for both conduct and ability. Not surprisingly, the good conduct did not last long, for as quickly as he got paid off he "found out the greatest difficulty in this life — how a newly landed sailor learns to pass the first saloon, and I never did fathom it." As fate would have it, the *Mermaid*'s next voyage was to run guns to Alaskan sealers, something frowned upon by the Russians, and the boat and crew were never seen again.

A year-and-a-half of being footloose and broke while seeing some of western North America was by this time beginning to wear a little thin and, not surprisingly, Jimmy found his thoughts drifting back to the blue mountains and some of the real men he had met there. Consequently, he headed back to the Canadian Rockies and the town of Banff, where his idol Peyto resided and where an interesting individual by the name of Tom Wilson, who he had met in 1896, had once offered him a job on the trail. His introduction to the town was "without the ringing of bells of welcome," but he quickly realized that he had made the right choice:

One summer morning I was strolling down the main street when I saw a group of horses being tied up at the hitching rail outside Dave White's store. They were pack ponies from Tom Wilson's corral which was just over the road where the Imperial Bank is now. The packers were supposed to be getting them ready to take a party of tourists in to Mt. Assiniboine. After tying up the ponies the packers went off for a drink, leaving the tourists sitting hopefully on the hitching rail. Time passed and the packers still weren't back. At last, around 4 o'clock, they returned, loaded themselves, and began struggling to load the horses with sacks of flour and sugar, every rope looking like six. An old Scotsman, who was watching them fumble, lost patience, whisked off his hat and hit the nearest pack pony over the head, shouting "Get to h— out of here!" The horses reared and then dashed across the road, taking the hitching rail and the tourists with them and busting the flour sacks all over the packers. The ponies fetched up in the minister's garden, where they ate up all his geraniums. I decided then and there that Banff was the place for me.

CHAPTER TWO

A Diamond in the Rough

Jimmy could not have arrived on the Banff scene at a more propitious moment, for Tom Wilson was just beginning to reap the benefits of an onslaught of American and overseas tourist-explorers and was hiring a number of his ilk. Many, like Bill Peyto, were immigrants from the British Isles, and "ninety percent of them were the same, just as though they had been carved from the same tree." Wilson himself had seen much of the west's history firsthand. Originally from Barrie, Ontario, he joined the North West Mounted Police in 1880 and served at Fort Walsh until 1881, when he joined Major A. B. Rogers, Engineer-in-Charge of the Mountain Section of Canadian Pacific Railway construction, as a packer. His exploits in the mountains included the discovery of both Lake Louise and Emerald Lake in 1882 and a solo trip on foot through Howse Pass to scout a possible location for the rail line. From 1883 onward he prospected some of the areas adjacent to the new CPR line in the mountains, joined Steele's Scouts to fight in the Northwest Rebellion and then was present at the historic driving of the railway's last spike at Craigellachie in November, 1885.

Given his knowledge of the mountains, it was not surprising that Wilson would put it to good use after the completion of the CPR. By 1887 the railway was busily engaged in developing the regions around Banff and Lake Louise for tourism and needed someone familiar with the area to blaze some trails and then accompany the early tourists over them. Wilson was their man, and soon he had established his corrals and outfitting headquarters on the busy corner of Buffalo Street and Banff Avenue, from whence his pack trains made their way into the mountain wilderness. His customers included some of the elite of the American mountaineering fraternity, such as Walter D. Wilcox and Charles E.

Fay, and they were followed by the British, such as J. Norman Collie and Hugh E. M. Stutfield, all of whom were anxious to attach their names to the first ascents of the big peaks that could be reached by pack train from the rail line. In addition, before long some of the foremost sportsmen in North America and from overseas heard of the excellent fish and game available in the mountains, and they too sought Wilson's services to outfit their sporting expeditions.

Obviously, anyone seeking work with Wilson had to have a fair knowledge of horses. When he arrived in Banff in 1898, Jimmy was somewhat deficient in this regard, and set about remedying the situation:

My next exploit in colonization was "topping off a horse." I had never ridden a horse other than a wooden one when six years old, but I was now in the west and it had to be done or lose face. The horse was tied in a clump of poplars down below the school house and quite a few spectators were on hand. I wondered why the man holding the horse had it gripped by the nostrils with his left hand and by its left ear with his right. I know now. I climbed into the saddle like a sailor climbing up the hind leg of a camel and heard someone yell, "let him go!" He meant the horse — and he went. So did I. A leaning poplar tree took me on the chest, under the chin, and I was in a bunch of scrub brush, head down. Other than a skinned cheek and a limp I was all right, but they did not get that horse for three days, five miles east and minus the bridle.

Jimmy persevered and quickly picked up the basics of riding, but it was not the only skill connected with horses that he needed, for the life of a trailman required a variety of aptitudes. One of the most important was to be able to properly pack a horse. All equipment, foodstuffs and other essentials of a pack train party had to be carried on the backs of the sure-footed mountain ponies, known as "cayuses," attached to a wooden pack saddle with a series of ropes looped around in a maze-like configuration and tied off with the famous diamond hitch. Much of this Jimmy picked up from a man who had been responsible for 160 head of horses while working for the U. S. Government in Alaska, but his main teacher was Tom Lusk. Lusk, like many in Wilson's employ, had a colourful background, sure to impress the "dudes" when out on the trail, and even the younger members of the crew like Jimmy:

He got across the Canadian border with a bunch of somebody's cattle and started ranching on his own. He was Tom Wilson's head guide when I first knew him, but his neighbors got suspicious when some of his cows gave birth to three or four calves a year, so he had to slide back to Texas in a hurry. He died coming back to Canada. He taught me much, but it was not ranching his way.

It was apparently Lusk who showed Jimmy a variation of the diamond hitch, the three-quarter diamond, which was quicker to throw, and he would use this knot for his entire guiding career.

Another useful asset for making a living on the trail was the ability to cook. The success of most tourist expeditions, after the care of the horses, depended on the ability of the trail cook to keep the party happy. From the hearty breakfast at the crack of dawn to the snack of bannock around the evening campfire, the cook was constantly called upon to fill the endless culinary yearnings that the hard physical life of the trail engendered. Fortunately for Jimmy, although his riding and packing abilities initially left something to be desired, he was a good cook, and that was why Wilson was willing to take him on.

The first party to which Jimmy was assigned was more of a group camp than a typical pack train party. It consisted of fourteen Philadelphians camped at Emerald Lake who took short day rides in the vicinity of the lake under the watchful eye of one of Wilson's main guides, Bob Campbell. Nonetheless, something came out of it that was very useful for Jimmy's future. Among the party were a Dr. Charles Schäffer, a medical doctor interested in botany, and his much younger, artistically inclined wife Mary Sharples Schäffer. At this early date, Mrs. Schäffer was not overly enamoured with camping in the mountains, although she had been adventuresome enough to ride from Banff to Laggan on top of a CPR locomotive, but that would change in the future. After the death of her husband, she would become one of the foremost explorers of the the unknown reaches of the Canadian Rockies and a close friend and admirer of Jimmy's, who she would provide with many important contacts for his business. The party also included three members of another important Philadelphia family, William, George and Mary Vaux, who had already been actively carrying out glacier surveys and measurement in the Selkirks for some time. They too would become part of the core of supporters upon whom Jimmy's livelihood would eventually depend.

Another interesting party that Jimmy was assigned to in 1898 consisted of two other ladies, a Miss Brunstermann and Agnes Laut, a noted Canadian historian who wrote several books on the Hudson's Bay Company, including *Lords of the North* and *Heralds of Empire*. These ladies proved more ambitious, spending some of their time in the vicinity of Emerald Lake, where the CPR was busily engaged in cutting trails, and then exploring north of Laggan where Jimmy took them "over the sloughs as far as Hector Lake." Afterwards, he accompanied them to the recently discovered Moraine Lake in the Valley of the Ten Peaks; they were among the first tourists to visit this famous beauty spot, and in this case he had to cut a rough trail himself to allow them to gain access.

At the time, Jimmy regarded these two outings to be of little consequence, and was therefore pleased when he was assigned to a real trail trip later in the year. This was a party from Richmond, Virginia out for a one month's pleasure trip north of Banff. Tom Wilson performed the guiding duties himself and Jimmy once again was assigned to cook. The party consisted of a brother and sister and a young doctor in attendance on the boy, who was tubercular. The trip, which went from Hillsdale, over Badger Pass, to the North Fork of the Cascade River and on to Sawback Lake, was intended to be of therapeutic value to the sickly youth, but it didn't work out that way. Soon after they returned to Virginia, word arrived in Banff that the boy had passed away. Jimmy mused, "Maybe it was my cooking that took what starch he had in him up among the angels, even though the doctor put on weight on the trip." In any event, Wilson didn't blame it on him.

At the end of the 1898 season, Jimmy took stock of his new occupation and decided that he liked it. Rather than leaving in the fall as he had done before, he decided to stay for the winter and give the trail a try again the next summer, perhaps hoping to be posted to some of Wilson's longer trips. His initial forays into the wilderness had intrigued him —

the high peaks, the sparkling lakes and tarns, the wild animals and all manner of wonders never even imagined by a young English lad. The Canadian Rockies had begun to take the hold on him that they would never release.

For the next few seasons, Jimmy continued to work for Wilson and to improve his trail skills. His knowledge of horses picked up gradually; he figured out how to tell one end from the other because the boys "used to tell me I was the east part of a horse going west." Soon, though, his familiarity with the vagaries of equine behaviour "came naturally to me, as though I had been at it all my life."

Because firearms were an integral part of life in the wilderness, he also had to improve on the skills learned with the small calibre weapons he had used to poach on the Marquis' estate in England. After he "blew the rim off my hat with an old 44 rifle" when he dropped it, he learned how to properly handle larger weapons. The game in the Canadian Rockies on which they were to be used was somewhat unique, consisting of deer, grizzly and black bear, bighorn sheep and mountain goat. Although Jimmy eventually became one of the foremost big game guides in Canada, particularly noted for his skill as a bighorn sheep hunter, knowledge of the habits and the territory of these animals did not come without a great deal of experience .

An opportunity to gain some important familiarity with both horses and big game hunting was not long in coming for Jimmy. Sportsmen in search of the fairly plentiful game of the Rockies formed a significant part of Wilson's business in the fall months. Usually these were business and professional men from the United States and Great Britain who could afford to pay for their pleasures and would book for longer periods of time than the average summer client. Such were the two "dudes," as the clients were referred to, that he was assigned to accompany as cook and hunting guide under head guide Ralph Edwards in October, 1899. Messrs. Parker and Twyford were Englishmen intent on probing part of the area north of Lake Louise that Wilson believed contained an abundance of virtually untouched game. This was to be Jimmy's first hunting trip, an important milestone.

The party's destination was the region around Wilcox Pass, the main link between the headwaters of the Saskatchewan and Athabasca Rivers and the route bypassing the recently discovered Columbia Icefield. Wilson had supplied guides Tom Lusk and Fred Stephens to American mountaineer and explorer Walter D. Wilcox for an examination of the headwaters of the Saskatchewan in 1896, leading to the discovery of the pass that bore Wilcox's name. Two years later, in 1898, Bill Peyto led another Wilson-outfitted party, consisting of British mountaineers Dr. J. Norman Collie, Hugh E. M. Stutfield and Hermann Woolley, to the same area, resulting in the discovery of the Columbia Icefield. Apart from its magnificent scenery, both these parties had reported on the abundance of game in the area, particularly bighorn sheep, leading Wilson to choose it for his English clients.

The route to Wilcox Pass followed up the Bow River to its headwaters, across the North Saskatchewan River onto its north fork, and then northward to its source. North of Laggan, the first stretch of trail was already beginning to gain a well-deserved bad reputation, which would only worsen as the years went by because of its muskegs and downed timber. Jimmy was fully familiar with this piece of trail for he had, in fact, helped to clear it in the spring of 1898 when he first went to work for Wilson. The outfitter had secured a contract from the CPR to construct a trail and Jimmy had been placed in charge as foreman over two other trailhands, Jim Tabuteau and Frank McNichol. The work was hard, requiring as it did numerous crossings of the river and the chopping of myriads of trees, but Jimmy was rewarded with an important "discovery" of his own. As the trail was pushed past Hector Lake and around the massive promontory of Bow Peak, where the valley narrowed to half its former width, the crew came upon the outlet of Bow Lake, its western shore exhibiting two fine glaciers, the Crowfoot and the Bow, cascading down steep mountain faces and disgorging their meltwater into the lake's sparkling blue waters.

Against the clear blue of a mountain sky it was a sight that impressed all three, but for Jimmy it was a revelation. He described it as "the most beautiful thing I'd seen in Canada." From the outlet they made their way around the marshy shoreline, sometimes preferring to travel on the gravel of the lake bed instead of the muskegy shore, and eventually camped at the north end beside a stream coursing through higher, timbered ground. Right then and there Jimmy fell in love with their campsite and thought, "I'll build a shack here sometime."

The Parker-Twyford party camped at the same site, allowing Jimmy to renew his acquaintance with his favourite spot. From there a few more days of hard travel brought them to Wilcox Pass, but the sheep that had reportedly been so abundant in the area were nowhere to be seen. In fact, the party was unsuccessful in shooting any game, much to the disappointment of the two Englishmen, who had even gone to the trouble of bringing an elephant gun in expectation of using it on grizzly bears. Instead it was relegated to use for target practice, and when Jimmy tried it out he received a rude shock. Taking aim at a tin can placed on a stump, he mistakenly pulled both triggers on the double-barrelled weapon at once and found himself on the seat of his pants six feet back of where he had been standing. He recalled that his shoulder was black and blue for a month.

Although the party didn't shoot any grizzly bears, one came close to their camp, resulting in its near destruction. The incident was described by guide Ralph Edwards in his entertaining book *The Trail to the Charmed Land*:

We were camped at the head of Wilcox Pass one night and were just getting settled in the dudes' tent for our usual little evening poker session when there was a peculiar, shrill squeal from the group of cayuses who, a few seconds before, had been peacefully feeding a scant few hundred yards away. There was a thunder of hooves, and as one pony, the whole bunch came flying madly, helter, skelter in our direction. I never saw ponies move so fast! Before we could make a move to get to our feet, the cayuses were in camp, tripping over tent guy ropes and stumbling over piles of saddles and other gear. Why they did not run right over us into the tent is something that I will never know, for they were absolutely crazy with fear, but as soon as they reached us they stopped suddenly, their sides heaving, their ears laid back, eyes literally standing out from their heads, and showing every symptom of horrified dread that an animal is capable of.

An examination of the meadow the next morning revealed the unmistakable tracks of a huge grizzly bear, whose scent had undoubtedly spooked the horses into the near fatal stampede. Edwards said the incident was his first experience with "the terror that a grizzly could inspire in the hearts of horses," and undoubtedly it was Jimmy's too. Both men stored the information away to become part of the future encyclopedic knowledge of the wilderness that their livelihood, and sometimes their lives, would depend upon.

While this important trip would stick out in Jimmy's mind for 1899, it was one of quite a different nature that would provide the highlight for the following year. During preparations to go out with a trail party in the summer of 1899, he had seen Walter Wilcox and his companions Henry G. Bryant and Louis J. Steele leave for Mount Assiniboine with Bob Campbell as guide. The Matterhorn-like Mount Assiniboine, the highest peak south of the CPR, had for several years been a challenging beacon to alpinists interested in important first ascents. One of the earliest trips outfitted and guided by Wilson, in 1893, had seen him take Chicago businessman Robert L. Barrett to its vicinity for an exploration they hoped would lead to a mountaineering attempt. Barrett was unable to try an ascent, and in 1895 he was back with Wilcox, again finding the going pretty rough. Assiniboine repelled Wilcox again during the 1899 trip, leaving it available for a party that Jimmy accompanied as cook in 1900.

The three would-be alpinists were Willoughby and English Walling from Chicago and a Montreal artist named Farrell. It would seem that they were a rather inexperienced lot. Wilson arranged not only for the services of his men, but also for three climbing guides to assist in gaining the prize. Because of the appearance of numerous alpinists in the Canadian Rockies and the death of one of them, Philip Abbot, on Mount Lefroy in 1896, the CPR brought two Swiss climbing guides, Edward Feuz and Christian Hasler, to the Rockies in 1899. They proved popular and the original guides were supplemented by several others the following year. The trip to Assiniboine was the first outing for two of them, Henry Zurfluh and Charles Clarke, who accompanied Feuz, but it was a less than auspicious debut.

During the trek to the foot of Assiniboine the artist Farrell asked Edward Feuz to take care of his watercolour box for him. Feuz promptly lost it, claiming he could not be expected to take care of it and the schnapps at the same time. This meant Farrell could not do any painting, and as he was not interested in climbing he stayed in camp and shot ducks while the others were off on the heights. When the party made its attempt on the peak, the climbing went well at first, but when they got to a band of rocks crossing west to east just below the summit, the guides decided to turn back. This, Jimmy felt, was unecessary: "The guides said the rifle vibrations of the artist at the lake was starting small avalanches & it was too dangerous. It might have been, but with three Swiss guides I think possibly they were indifferent climbers."

After their failure, the Wallings decided to return to Banff as quickly as possible and the pack train made its way back via Bryant Creek and the Spray River. As Jimmy reported it, the end of the trip was to prove as much a fiasco as the mountaineering, after he turned back with the pack horses because of the downed timber:

That is the party that got lost trying to get to the CPR hotel via the Spray River; got lost, killed a saddle horse for meat within fifty yards of a lumber road & were found the next day. The three guides made the hotel that night, then reported the lost party next morning. The packtrain had to turn back & go via Canmore as it would have taken a week to cut through via the Spray River.

To make up for their bad luck, and probably as a public relations gesture, Wilson sent the Wallings on a week's "recovery trip" from Banff to Laggan. Tom Lusk was the guide and Jimmy once more went along as cook, but again things didn't work out as the outfitter had hoped: "The two boys liked Blackberry brandy, took two bottles & while I had them hunting, old Tom polished off all the brandy & was well baked when we got back to camp." There is no record of the Walling brothers ever returning to the Canadian Rockies, something every outfitter, including Jimmy himself in later years, had to face after a trip where everything seemed to go wrong.

If the Walling expedition was a case of nothing going the way it should, Jimmy's next major outing, in 1902, was just the opposite. That year he accompanied one of the day's foremost alpinists, the Reverend James Outram, on one of the most successful mountaineering expeditions ever accomplished in the Canadian Rockies. In doing so, he went a long way to establishing the reputation as a guide that would be critical to the success of his own guiding and outfitting business in the years ahead.

The circumstances of this trip were quite different from his previous work as a cook for Wilson. Tom was busily engaged in attempting to get the outfitting concessions for the CPR hotels at Field and Lake Louise in the period after the turn of the century, something he achieved early in 1902. Because the railroad company was interested in having secure services available at all its hotels, that left the field at Banff open and there, for the moment at least, Jimmy's old acquaintance Bill Peyto was in the ascendancy. Peyto had left Banff to fight in the Boer War with Lord Strathcona's Horse in 1900 and had returned a local hero early in 1901. At that point he had decided to go into the outfitting game on his own, and was successful in attracting the most famous mountaineer of the day, Sir Edward Whymper, the conqueror of the Matterhorn, to utilize his services for an expedition under the auspices of the CPR in 1901. This particular venture did not last long, as the two Englishmen frequently locked horns, but later that summer Peyto had quickly and successfully taken James Outram to the foot of the oft-tried Mount Assiniboine, where the reverend gentleman gained success.

Although Jimmy probably continued to work for Wilson in 1901, when Peyto requested his services to assist with a new and far-reaching expedition planned by Outram for 1902, he was happy to accept. His friendship with and admiration for Peyto had grown since he had come to Banff, and he was a frequent visitor to Bill's outfitting shack and corrals on the riverbank off Bear Street. Bill was an inveterate prospector and his partner and companion in these ventures was an Australian, Jack Sinclair. In later life Jimmy would write an article about his "hero" Peyto and would recall a visit he made to the shack about 1899:

When I visited their shack they had just tossed a coin as to who would enlist in the Boer War or stay and look after their copper claims and keep them in good standing. Bill won, so he would join Sam Steeles' regiment and go to war. The "Aussie" would stay in Banff, but being a gold prospector he had no real love for base metals. On this visit he was fusing together fine gold fathered in New Guinea with a glowpipe and charcoal. I was fascinated; what kid would not be. Real gold in an Australian pickle bottle, heavy, dull yellow and very real. To these two, the operation seemed only routine but to me, well, you can guess.

As for Peyto, he was obviously impressed with the progress that had been made by the green "kid" who had first visited him in his tent at Laggan in 1896 — in fact, so much so that he decided to place him in charge of the expedition, since the pressure of his new business required his presence in Banff during much of the period of Outram's outing. Jimmy would not misplace the confidence put in him.

The "dude" for the trip, the Reverend James Outram, was an interesting study. At one time he had been the Vicar of St. Peter's, Ipswich, but he had come to Canada, where his brother apparently already lived, for reasons of health in 1900. Outram had climbed in Switzerland and had a philosophy of mountains that combined an appreciation of their natural beauty with the more lofty ideals of his calling: "There is a wonderful fascination about mountains. Their massive grandeur, majesty of lofty height, splendour of striking outline — crag and pinnacle and precipice — seem to appeal both to the intellect and to the innermost soul of man, and to compel a mingled reverence and love." But he admitted to a more prosaic concern that drew him away from Switzerland and brought him to the wilds of Canada: "But though its scenery is unchangingly beautiful and the familiar Alpine monarchs retain forever the affection of the mountaineer, yet his soul will crave — and rightly so — the chief joy of the climber's ambition, a 'first ascent'." This admission would cause Outram some difficulty with his fellow alpinists — Dr. J. Norman Collie for one calling him an "interloper" and expressing the opinion that some of those who had done the earlier exploration in the range should "get some of the scalps." This attitude may account for the fact that Outram was unaccompanied by other mountaineers on his 1902 trip.

At the source of the West Branch of the North Fork of the Saskatchewan River, now known as the Alexandra River but for a period referred to by some as the "Nashan River" in Jimmy's honour, lay the area Outram was interested in. The mountains that had caught his attention included Columbia, Forbes, Freshfield, Bryce and Lyell, all of which he had glimpsed from summits he had ascended further south in 1900 and 1901. Apparently he had convinced the CPR to provide at least partial support for his venture, as he was given the services of Swiss guide Christian Kaufmann free of charge. It seems likely that Peyto's outfitting services might also have been at least partially subsidized as well, since Outram had no visible means of support at the time.

Jimmy's involvement with the expedition began well in advance of the actual pack trip in July. He and a fellow worker, Fred Ballard, were given the task of clearing some of the trail the trip was to follow. Ballard was a rough-and-tumble product of the Michigan woods who had come to Banff about 1900 and had also worked for Wilson for a period. His most ambitious outing to date had been in 1901 as the cook with Professor Jean Habel, a German mathematics professor who had climbed in the Rockies since 1896. The objective of the expedition had been to explore the famous fur trade route over Athabasca Pass, and even though they failed to reach it they did accomplish a detailed examination of the Fortress Lake area. Jimmy described Ballard as "no diplomat" and related that he and Habel had tangled frequently during the trip. Habel had been constantly searching for the blazes of the earlier A. P. Coleman party in his quest for Athabasca Pass, and when Ballard heard a short time after the trip that Habel had died suddenly his response was, "Good, he can see the blazes now." Despite his idiosyncracies, Peyto knew that Ballard, with his Michigan background, was a strong man with an axe and was also one of the best trail cooks to be found in Banff, attributes that were going to be much in demand on this trip.

As soon as the trails were dry enough in the spring, Jimmy and Ballard set out on horseback to the area between Bow Lake and the mouth of the Mistaya River, where the winter's ravages had left the trail littered with downed timber. The country was not new to the two axemen, for they had spent the previous winter on a trapline in the area. By this time Jimmy himself was no slouch with an axe either, having spent the winter of 1900 with fellow Englishman and packer Ross Peacock in the upper Bow Valley taking out timber and floating it downstream for sale to a sawmill near Kananaskis. Before they had finished their chore, he and Ballard had cleared more than three hundred trees baring the route to the north and had picked out some locations to build cabins on for the next winter's proposed trapline.

The trip, planned to take two months, began at Laggan on July 9th and, because Outram was aware that previous expeditions north of the Saskatchewan River had run short of supplies and had suffered "privations more or less severe," there was an abundance of supplies. Outram's list, from his book *In the Heart of the Canadian Rockies*, gives a good picture of what a typical trail party would carry and what Jimmy, as a packer, would have to deal with on a daily basis:

The provisions, to commence with the most important items, consisted of a mainstay of flour and bacon; canned goods of various descriptions, including milk, corn, tongues, boneless turkey and other birds, beef, and jam; sugar, salt and other seasonings; baking-powder, dried fruits — apples, pears, prunes, apricots and raisins; rice and oatmeal, cheese and chocolate, tea, coffee, cocoa, and a varied assortment of soups about complete the tale, and we fared sumptuously every day. Two small tents accommodated the four of us, bestowed in pairs; blankets and sleeping bags, according to individual taste, completed the night equipment; kitchen and table utensils, strictly limited to bare necessities, made up the camp furniture. Our personal baggage varied from the little more than change of raiment of my three companions to my own dittos, stuffed into a common sack, together with my solitary luxury (an air mattress and pump) and sundry instruments required for semi-scientific purposes; and four ice-axes formed a most harassing climax to the number of the packs.

Peyto assisted in the early stages of the trip where the trails were particularly bad and where fourteen horses were required to get the supplies to a location where some of them could be cached. Again, Outram supplied a good picture of what the start of a trip looked like from a dude's point of view:

It is just 7.20, but each day sees the routine of packing more nearly perfected and the time occupied in getting under way grows less and less. Peyto leads on his well-tried black mare, followed by the string of pack—horses, which make occasional dashes for the leadership, shaking up their packs and bumping into one another or any trees that they can hit. The packing and the "hitch" are early and most fully tested. In the middle of the bunch comes Fred, and Jim brings up the rear; both have considerable "driving" to do, as the commencement of a march invariably calls for some discipline and training: some of the cayuses were new to pack-train work, and all were on their first trip of the season and apt to be a little slow and contrary, until they got into good condition and their regular routine of place and method was established.

An average day's ride lasted about six hours and after the camp was made in mid-afternoon Outram and Kaufmann spent their time taking pictures or doing minor explorations of the next day's route. Often there was a trail for the men to cut, but where there was not Jimmy and Fred would "disport themselves in a leisurely fashion." At certain locations they would also take the opportunity to construct rough cabins for use on the planned winter trapline and Outram noted that two or three of them "stood as memorials of afternoons off and days when Christian and I were on the heights."

One of these cabins, near the mouth of the Mistaya River, was used to cache the extra supplies, and after helping get the horses across the North Saskatchewan, Peyto prepared to return to Banff with three of the pack horses. On taking his leave he turned to Jimmy and said, "Well, now you're on your own," little realizing how prophetic his words were. No longer was he the cook, nor the packer; now he was the guide, and that's the position he would retain for the remainder of his career.

Outram intended to ascend some of the mountains around the headwaters of the Alexandra River and decided to begin with Mount Columbia, one of the most striking mountains in the Canadian Rockies. After trailing up the river the pack train took to the woods where, Outram noted, "the good work done by our two axemen enabled us to traverse the thick forest with ease" and allowed them to make camp within striking distance of the mountain. However, while making camp, Jimmy and Fred became careless and had a close call:

The packs had just been unloaded and their contents were lying scattered all around; Kaufmann and I were busy putting up one of the tents, and

Fred was engaged in preparing a well-earned dinner, when suddenly a crackling sound was heard and I looked up to see the lowest branch of a young balsam fir close to the fire ablaze. In an instant a sheet of flame swept to the topmost bough with a rushing hiss and crackle like a monster rocket, and the entire tree became a blazing pillar of fire. Another and another caught, the lurid flames shot up like fireworks, and thousands of burning spines fell all around in showers. A general rush was made to rescue our belongings from the circle of fiery rain, whilst the prospect of a raging forest fire, devastating this beautiful virgin valley, was imminent. Fortunately the breeze, whose variable eddies blew first this way and then that in our secluded corner, veered just at this crisis and set steadily towards the boulder-covered flat. The flames died down, and the trees, dry as tinder, that circled the three other sides, were spared. Water was close at hand, and soon the smouldering blankets, tents, packmantles, garments and saddlery were safe from further destruction, although riddled with holes from the fall of blazing sparks and looking rather dilapidated during the remainder of the trip.

The incident provided a valuable lesson for Jimmy and thereafter he was always extremely careful in placing the campfire, recognizing that such a mistake could destroy his livelihood.

The danger past, Jimmy accompanied Outram and Kaufmann on a late-afternoon reconnaisance of the giant Mount Columbia. It was an exhausting trek that required the three to travel over seemingly interminable miles of crevasse-pocked glacier. The enthusiasm of the two mountaineers was infectious and, after joining them on this outing and seeing the way to the summit, Jimmy asked Outram if he could accompany them on the morrow. Outram refused, a slight Jimmy would never forgive or forget, and the first ascent was made only by the "Herren" and his Swiss guide. Later Jimmy would say, "Outram wanted all the glory himself," and claimed that he treated his guide Kaufmann as "just help." But he did not have to wait long to get his revenge. A short time after his success on Columbia, Outram moved on for an attempt on Mount Lyell, the keystone peak of the region. Because he had a lot of surveying and photographic instruments he wanted to get to the summit to accurately record the area, he asked Jimmy to accompany the climb and carry some of this equipment. Jimmy politely declined.

Despite this disagreement, the trip proved a tremendous success. After his achievements at the head of the Alexandra, including the first ascent of Mount Bryce, Outram joined Dr. J. Norman Collie's party for a spate of climbing further south, including the first ascent of Mount Forbes. On the way back to Banff he and Kaufmann also completed the first traverse of Mount Wilson, while Jimmy and Fred brought the pack train around the base of the massive peak. In all, during the 54 days of the expedition, Outram participated in the first ascents of 10 major peaks, and achieved all his objectives. The reputation he had sought as an important pioneer climber in the Canadian Rockies was now secure, and Outram was well pleased. Therefore, he was most laudatory in his remarks about Jimmy in his book, published in 1905. Soon it was being read by many others who were anxious to climb, hunt or explore in this new and interesting region, and were equally keen to know of a tried and tested guide who could take them there. For many, Jimmy became their man.

CHAPTER THREE

Branching Out

When asked in later years how he got started in the outfitting business, Jimmy had a standard reply: "I cabled our English lawyers that I had passed my twenty-first birthday ten minutes ago to get the legacy coming to me on that date from some relative I never knew, who in a moment of weakness left it thus, over to Canada immediately, if not sooner. It went into horses and saddlery bought from old Frank Ricks of Morley and I started into packtrains and have done it ever since." Jimmy never explained who the relative was, but it is clear he knew for some time that he would receive this legacy when he reached his majority. If his recollection was accurate, the money would have arrived late in 1898 and he would have begun to buy his stock in 1899. However, there is no evidence that he immediately began to take out parties on his own, apparently preferring to combine his pack string with someone else's, as he probably did on the Outram trip. But after that historic expedition it is clear that he resolved to start his own outfitting business.

Even at that, he began cautiously. In the years after the completion of the railway, the Dominion government was active in surveying the new lands that the line had opened up in western Canada. The mountains were no exception, and in 1886 J. J. McArthur, a Dominion Land Surveyor, was appointed to begin a topographic survey of the Rockies using a new technique utilizing cameras to take views from high mountain stations. Tom Wilson had packed for several survey parties when starting his business, and Jimmy was astute enough to see there were benefits to getting established in this way. The Dominion Topographic Survey was still active in its phototopographic work and in 1903 he contracted his services to the government and accompanied a party of surveyors assigned to work between the railway and the North Saskatchewan River. Heading up the crew was Arthur O. Wheeler, D.L.S., who had just spent an exhausting two years surveying the rugged Selkirk Range, where the woods were thick and the mountains high. Part way through the first year his assistants found the work so difficult that they quit, and Wheeler had been given two new men, his brother Hector Wheeler and Morrison P. Bridgland, to complete the work. It was this same crew that Jimmy was assigned to assist.

The summer consisted of packing the survey camp from the base of one peak to another and then setting up to allow the surveyors maximum comfort when they were not on the heights engaged in their work. Since the survey equipment was heavy, consisting of a bulky 20 pound camera and plates as well as a 15 pound transit and other instruments, Jimmy was occasionally asked to help. Because the waiting could become rather tedious, he was quite happy to have the opportunity for some exercise. During the season, he accompanied the surveyors to the tops of two peaks, Mount Niblock near Lake Louise and Cirque Peak to the north of Dolomite Pass, his first recorded mountaineering ascents.

Jimmy's acquaintance with A. O. Wheeler was a particularly important one, as the strong-minded and capable surveyor was on his way to becoming one of the most important individuals in the Canadian Rockies. In fact, it was likely Wheeler who introduced him to his future partner and it may have been he who suggested they combine forces. The chief packer for Wheeler in the Selkirks during 1901 and 1902 had been a Yorkshireman named George Taylor, who had spent some time ranching before joining Wheeler's survey. After completing the work, he had been successful, perhaps with Wheeler's influence, in gaining the newly-let concession for outfitting and guiding services at Glacier House, the railway's famous alpine hotel near the foot of the Illecillewaet Glacier in Rogers Pass. Although the details of their agreement are not known, Jimmy and he had begun to work together as Simpson and Taylor by early 1904. Perhaps Jimmy intended to combine forces with him at Glacier, an area he was certainly familiar with from his bridge work with the CPR. If so, plans changed and he continued to run the Banff end of the business while Taylor took care of the Glacier end. In any event, the partnership did not last long, for Taylor soon decided to go back into the ranching game. Taking over the Glacier operation in

1905 was Jimmy's close friend and assistant Sydney Baker, who would ultimately go on to establish an interesting reputation of his own in the Selkirks.

Baker had apprenticed as a surveyor in his native Suffolk and after fighting in the Boer War, he, like many fellow young Englishmen, decided to see some more of the world. After arriving in Canada he worked as a cook on some prairie ranches before visiting Banff and deciding that the mountains were the life for him. As an outdoorsman who immediately became capable at both summer and winter wilderness travel, it was inevitable that he and Jimmy would soon become fast friends. In fact, Jimmy had looked no further for an assistant when taking out his first important party in 1904.

By the time Jimmy began his own outfitting and guiding business, he had taken several steps in addition to acquiring the horses and saddlery that were necessary for a successful career. Most important was the establishment of a headquarters in Banff. In 1903 Jimmy was successful in acquiring a vacant lot (Lot 8, Block A) next to his friend Peyto's cabin and corrals along the Bow River near Buffalo Street. It was an ideal location, close to downtown but at the same time near the quiet of the river and a good source of water for his horses. He quickly set to work to build a small cabin as a residence and some corrals for his horses.

The other necessity, which he acquired with equal ease, could best be characterized as the "mystique" of the mountain guide. Again taking his cue from Peyto, who Walter Wilcox had at one time described as "wild and picturesque," he had adorned his short and wiry frame with all the accoutrements that his dudes would expect of a mountain cowboy. These included a rough buckskin shirt with fringes worn over khaki pants, somewhat dilapidated from trail wear, and, crowning his full head of reddish hair, a pony stetson like those worn by the Mounted Police. Jimmy claimed he chose this particular hat because of its stiff brim, which the wind would not blow over his field glasses when he was spotting game. Complementing his outfit was a ready smile, sparkling blue eyes and a quick wit that kept his guests constantly at ease. Accompanying him as a bosom companion was his trail dog "Dooley," a black mongrel he had pulled out of a sack of puppies being taken to the river to be drowned. Topping this all off was a lifestyle that would be expected of one who spent so much time in the wilderness away from the pleasures of town.

Throughout his life, Jimmy loved to tell stories about his fondness for rum, or "Nelson's blood" as he called it, and his drinking exploits. When he later recalled the early days in the west he claimed: "This whole country was built on rum. Nobody drank any water when I came here. They all said the Good Lord made it for running under bridges. When you could buy Seagram '83 at $10 a case for twelve quarts who would drink water?" Some of his stories were undoubtedly apocryphal, but certainly in his early years the availability of cheap refreshment combined with his bachelor state led to many an all-night poker game and plenty of carousel with the other boys of the trail when the opportunity arose. During the earlier hours of the day, if someone was looking for him, they would be directed to the pool hall or the King Edward Hotel bar, his two favourite haunts.

Perhaps it was Jimmy's growing reputation as a "character," or as a competent mountain guide, or the fact that he was an Englishman, or the combination of all three that attracted his first real client. Mrs. Mary de la Beach-Nichol was somewhat eccentric in her own right. The daughter of Sir Michael Edward Hicks-Beach, the Viscount St. Aldwyn, Chancellor of the Exchequer in 1885-86 and again from 1895 to 1902, she had taken up lepidoptery late in life after raising a family of six children. Of substantial means, her avocation gained her a collection that ranked with such renowned collectors as the Rothschilds, and when she came to visit Canada from Wales she had been commissioned to collect for the British Museum. A tiny woman clad in an old black gown, her grey hair poking out from under a beat-up Panama hat, she was stone deaf and carried an ear trumpet everywhere. When she contacted Jimmy, he suggested a trip into some of the valleys neighbouring the railroad that might bear some hitherto uncollected varieties of butterflies or moths, and she accepted the suggestion. With Syd Baker as packer, he led her first to the Yoho Valley, then to the Lake O'Hara region and finally to the area around Mount Assiniboine. It was a unique experience, for he spent most of the summer with a butterfly net in his hands or carrying the collecting box behind her as she stalked her quarry.

The "butterfly lady," as Jimmy soon referred to her, was apparently well pleased with the services he had offered her, and she became one of his most faithful early clients. Returning for a second trip in 1905, she expressed the desire to explore some new, more arid surroundings where different varieties than those caught in 1904 might be found. A decision was made to search the area around Lake Okanagan and southward into the State of Washington. Since Syd Baker was now in charge of the Glacier operation, Jimmy had to turn elsewhere for an assistant, and again he found one in an extremely capable fellow Englishman. Sid Unwin was the nephew of one of England's leading publishers, T. Fisher Unwin, but he found England too constricting after returning from the Boer War and headed for Canada. Arriving in Banff in 1904, he had immediately befriended Syd Baker and had accompanied him on a trapping trip to the North Saskatchewan River that winter, leading to his employment by Simpson and Baker the following summer.

The 1905 trip, which would see the party penetrate as far south as Lake Chelan in Washington, was one of the most unique outings that Jimmy would ever lead. He began by shipping his horses by rail to Salmon Arm at the north end of the Okanagan Valley, after which he trailed them around Okanagan Lake, got them across the Similkameen River on a barge, and then went up the Ashnola River into rattlesnake country. Jimmy became concerned that because of his client's deafness she would not hear the snakes' warning rattle, but he soon realized that he needn't have worried:

We went out into the Bekaah Valley. The dear old Welsh lady was deaf as a post and she carried this big old brass trumpet in her hand which she put up to her ear when you were talking to her. But in the rattlesnake country she had no nerves at all. I would cut a little forked stick and she would go out into the long grass looking for rattlesnakes, pin one down by the back of the head with the forked stick, get out a pocket knife, cut its head off and bring it back to me to skin. And then she'd take them back to Wales as a souvenir.

On the return trip the party followed a different route, over a high pass onto the head of the Tulameen River and all the way down it to Princeton. As this had been planned in advance, the butterfly lady had requested that her mail be shipped to the post office there so she could pick it up. Because they arrived on a Sunday the post office, which was in a store, was closed up tight and Jimmy had to find the postmaster and ask if he could get some mail for Mrs. Beach-Nichol. "Oh no," said the postmaster, "it's strictly against regulations to open on a Sunday — it can't be done." "That's too bad," Jimmy retorted, "I was going to buy a bit of food as well." "Oh, well " said the postmaster, "that's a different matter — I'd open the store for 50 cents." He got the mail, all the food he wanted and "finally, I was invited into the hotel to get drunk."

It was during this trip that Jimmy luckily avoided a situation that could have quickly foreshortened his career, much as he had by not shipping out to run guns to the Alaskan sealers. While on the trail south of the Similkameen River, he ran into an uncleared stretch crossing the International Boundary. Needing some assistance, he hired a man he met who went by the name of Billy Dunn to help open it up. When the job was completed he paid Dunn off with some of the butterfly lady's money, and on taking his leave Dunn invited Jimmy to come back and meet him after he was finished with his party, claiming he had a scheme where they could both make some money. Jimmy thought about it for a while, but at the end of the trip decided to return to Banff and carry out his original plan to go trapping. When he heard the news the next spring, he thanked his lucky stars he had. Dunn, known more widely as Shorty Dunn, had joined forces with the famous outlaw Bill Miner and an itinerant schoolteacher named Louis Colquhoun to hold up the west-bound CPR Imperial Limited at Ducks, west of Revelstoke, in May, 1906. Six days later all three were captured by the Mounties and eventually sentenced to twenty years in prison. On musing over his meeting with Dunn, Jimmy said: "He knew that I knew enough about horses that I could take care of them while they were holding up the train. I wouldn't have known anything about it until they were actually doing it. Lucky again —I wasn't there."

Jimmy's third outing with the butterfly lady, in 1907, was not to be nearly so exciting, but it did allow her to complete her Canadian collections. This time he accompanied Mrs. Beach-Nichol to an area that he was now becoming extremely familiar with, the North Fork of the North Saskatchewan River and Wilcox Pass. During this trip they encountered the Mary Schäffer party, led by Billy Warren, a fellow English guide formerly in Wilson's employ. Schäffer's party was intent on finding a beautiful lake rumoured by the Indians to lie somewhere north of the Columbia Icefield. In her book *Old Indian Trails of the Canadian Rockies* Mrs. Schäffer paid Jimmy the ultimate compliment for his contribution to opening up this area of the wilderness and thereby aiding in their eventual discovery of Maligne Lake the following year:

As this chronicle now leads us up Nashan River, I might here give our apparently high-handed reason for changing the well-known or rather lengthy name of this river, printed on the present maps of that region as "West-Branch-of-the-North-Fork-of-the-Saskatchewan," to "Nashan," or, in full, Nashan-esen (Wolverine-go-quick). It is the Stoney-Indian name for our friend Jim Simpson, given him by his Indian admirers out of compliment to his speed in walking on snowshoes or off. Jim's axe in this country has done more to make the old trails passable for future comers than any others, and this little tribute to his labours seems small enough, — to name a beautiful valley and river for one who has helped to make a hard road easier.

Mary Schäffer's book would attract considerable attention, catching many readers' imagination with her story of an undaunted widow's exploration and discovery in the Rockies, and, as with Outram's book, the good words for Jimmy were of great benefit to him. As for Mrs. Beach-Nichol, she had discovered two new varieties of moths on her three trips, and thus was happy to also heartily recommend his services. Unfortunately, one individual she did send him was her nephew, John Blandy-Jenkins, who Jimmy called "the Millionaire Kid" and described as "being constantly on one's mind, and the main concern was when he was going to get off." Around 1910 he received a cable from Mrs. Beach-Nichol telling him to prepare for a four month hunting trip for four people starting June 1st. Before he had a chance to reply that all hunting was closed at that time of the year, young Blandy-Jenkins arrived with "a chauffeur, two jockeys and two trunks full of bowie knives and guns." On his way to the west he had stopped off in New York to marry a follies girl and it had cost him $25,000 to get rid of her. As Jimmy said, "for a new arrival he was doing very well," but of course he wasn't able to oblige him with a hunt. Afterwards, he heard that Blandy-Jenkins had unsuccessfully taken up ranching "with no stock, but plenty of sweet Burgundy" and had then gone on to break the hearts of numerous women. Jimmy speculated that he had ended up being "shot at sunrise somewhere by some outraged husband."

In the year before Jimmy's last trip with the butterfly lady, events were afoot in the Canadian Rockies that were to substantially affect him. With the great interest in climbing that was evident throughout the region, his former employer, A. O. Wheeler, had been attempting to emulate organizations in other mountainous countries and form an alpine club in Canada. Early in 1906 he was successful in convincing the CPR to provide twenty passes from anywhere on their line to get delegates to a founding meeting of the club in Winnipeg. Because he knew that any mountaineering club was going to rely heavily on the services of outfitters and guides, he made sure he invited a number of the Rocky Mountain guides to attend. He had many to choose from, since from 1902 onward there had been a large increase in the amount of competition on the outfitting and guiding scene. Most were men who, like Jimmy, had at one time worked for Tom Wilson and had then gone out on their own. They included Billy Warren, Tom Martin, Closson and Jack Otto, Fred Stephens and Bob Campbell. The latter had bought Wilson out in 1904 when he decided to turn his attention to raising horses and trading with the Indians from a small trading post he had established at the Kootenay Plains on the North Saskatchewan River. The one exception was the new company of Brewster Brothers, ultimately the largest competitor of all, which had been started by the two young sons of Banff dairyman John Brewster, Bill and Jim. With the infusion of some capital from their American brother-in-law Phil Moore, this company had successfully gained the CPR livery and outfitting concession at the Banff Springs Hotel in 1904. They would become Jimmy's chief rival for business and the object of much of his ire in the years ahead.

Because Jimmy was out trapping in March, 1906 when the Alpine Club of Canada's founding meeting was held in Winnipeg, his partner Syd Baker went to represent their interests. Several other guides and outfitters, including Bob Campbell, Tom Martin and Tom Wilson, were also in attendance. At the meeting it was decided that the focus of the club would be an annual mountaineering camp held at some appropriate location in the mountains where new members could be taught climbing skills on easy peaks while experienced ones tested theirs on more difficult ascents. For the inaugural camp, Summit Lake in the Yoho Valley was chosen as the site, and Wheeler asked that each outfitter donate some horses and their services free of charge to get the club off to a good start.

The idea worked; in July, 1906 the first week-long annual camp was held with 112 people in attendance. Simpson and Baker donated the use of some of their tents to house the participants and Syd Baker was present with about ten horses to assist in the job of getting members to and from the railroad at Field and taking them on short excursions around the Yoho Valley. Wheeler, who had been elected director of the club, was well pleased with the results, and immediately began to lay plans for a bigger and better affair the following summer. Each year thereafter the camp grew and there were better opportunities for the area's outfitters to participate in its benefits. For the 1908 camp, planned at Rogers Pass, Wheeler asked the Otto brothers, who had assisted him on the survey following Jimmy's stint in 1903, and Simpson and Baker to be the two main outfitters. He was so taken with their efficient handling of the situation that he decided the club needed an "Official Outfitter," and in 1909 the Otto brothers received this appointment. That year Jimmy and Syd Baker had decided to go their separate ways and Syd had bought out his interest in the Glacier operation. Now completely independent, Jimmy held discussions with Wheeler that resulted in his appointment as the Alpine Club's "Equerry," the Ottos' assistant in charge of horse transport. It was to be the beginning of a long relationship with the club that would bring him many new customers.

Jimmy began his new position by providing horse transport for the club camp held on the meadow bordering beautiful Lake O'Hara. Because of the distance from the railroad, this required a tremendous amount of packing, especially since 60 tents and copious supplies of food and other sundries were required to care for the needs of the 190 participants in attendance. For the first time, the packers were allotted their own section of the camp.

Wheeler was keen on having visitors from other countries' alpine clubs or famous climbers attend the club and address those present. This year he had successfully convinced the CPR to provide passage for the famous Edward Whymper to visit the Rockies one last time to attend the camp. As the most famous English mountaineer of the day, Whymper had made three previous visits under the CPR's auspices, in 1901, 1903 and 1904, in order to advertise the mountains. The results had been the topic of many a story. Already in his sixties, Whymper had tried the patience of almost every guide in the area and had been rumoured to have more of a thirst for hard liquor than climbing mountains.

Jimmy's recollection of Whymper fit the mould: "I never saw a man who could hold so much liquor — he drank enough to knock 12 men off their feet." One day shortly after the camp began, Jimmy went around to the various climber's tents to see if they had any mail they wished to have posted . On reaching Whymper's, he was asked inside, where the great man confided in him: "You know Simpson, this is the poorest bunch I've ever been with. I can't find anyone to help me drink my beer." Jimmy was happy to help him solve the problem and "from that point onward he had no trouble at all, I was there every time he opened one."

While packing up Whymper's baggage after he had made his speech and was preparing to leave camp, Jimmy was told to be very careful with one of the cartons. His suspicions aroused, he gave it a shake and heard it go "gurgle, gurgle, gurgle." Upon arriving at the CPR's Mount Stephen House in Field, Whymper invited him up to his room for a drink and, after pouring himself a huge tumbler of scotch, said: "Simpson, I had a very clever brother who drank himself to death . I used to say 'George, George, why don't you take it in moderation the same way I do.' " Given that Whymper had probably already polished off three bottles that morning Jimmy thought to himself, "My God, George must have been a good one."

In the final analysis, Jimmy was much taken with making Whymper's acquaintance and never forgot it. In his own inimitable fashion, he paid the mountaineer several compliments, once describing him as "such a cartoons of that dog standing astride the Union Jack ready to devour anyone who touched it." And despite his weaknesses, he found him to be tremendously effective: "He'd sit in camp and drink No. 4 Scotch all day and send his four crack Swiss guides to climb a mountain. When they came back to camp and reported he'd then sit down and write a damn fine article for the CPR."

After the completion of the camp, Wheeler had arranged for some of his English visitors and a few of the club's members to go on a six day hike around the Yoho Valley. Jimmy accompanied one of the Ottos with the pack train and duly impressed several of the participants with his abilities. One of them later described these in an article for the *Canadian Alpine Journal*:

Otto, the Club's Master of the Horse, was some way ahead in front of the string of horses, but his Equerry, Jimmy Simpson, riding last, proved a most entertaining and instructive companion. His control over the animals struck me as wonderful. When one of them went wrong he rated it, either by its individual name or by names (also used in England) of more general and forcible application; and the offender always returned promptly to the trail. At one point, a horse got stuck near the top of a steep and slippery pitch, and after many unsuccessful efforts to pull him up Jimmy said there was nothing for it but push him down. The poor brute fell a considerable distance and landed with his pack beneath him and legs in the air. He was soon righted, however, and then got up the pitch safely; but we both agreed that it had been odds he would break a leg in that fall.

The trip held a number of similar difficulties, and when next he saw Wheeler, Jimmy roundly condemned the whole enterprise as a hare-brained scheme. One of the climbing guides, Conrad Kain, reported that this had made the Director livid with rage, but Jimmy had not backed down. Wheeler soon cooled off, however, since if it had not been for Simpson's honesty the whole camp might have foundered.

Wheeler did not get along well with the Brewster company, as he felt they had left him in the lurch during the first Alpine Club, and the enmity was mutual. As the Brewsters were the CPR concessionnaires,

Wheeler complained to William Whyte, vice-president of the railway, describing the Brewsters' apparent attempt to obtain the valuable right to outfit the club camps:

Last summer we contracted with Otto Bros. to outfit the Alpine Club camp at Lake O'Hara. Otto Bros. told me they were short of horses and had made an arrangement to buy some from Tom Wilson. J. W. Otto asked me to see Wilson in the matter. This I did and he promised to help out Otto Bros. all he could, to supply the Alpine Club camp. Next, I learned from Otto that Wilson had sold the horses in question to Brewster. I thought nothing of this at the time. If Brewster offered better terms I presumed Wilson sold to him on that account. Later the action assumed more significance.

To carry out their contract with the Alpine Club, Otto Bros. had to employ Jimmy Simpson and his outfit of horses, some ten in number. After the camp was over J. W. Otto told me that Brewster had offered Simpson $300.00 to lose his horses so that they would not be available for the camp, but that Simpson had declined to break faith with Otto. Had the scheme been successful we should have been left badly in the lurch with a number of distinguished English alpine people on our hands and, naturally, I felt rather indignant.

Because of his integrity, Jimmy was still front and centre when plans were being laid for the next year's main Alpine Club camp at Consolation Lake and auxiliary camp in the Yoho Valley. And Wheeler again expressed his faith in him by recommending his services to the man who would be the distinguished English alpine guest for the 1910 camp, Dr. Thomas G. Longstaff. Longstaff's reputation as an alpinist was second only to Whymper's and had been mainly gained for his work among the giants of the Caucasus and Himalayas. When he arrived in the Rockies he set his sights on one of its grandest peaks, Mount Assiniboine.

The Longstaff party, which included his sister Katharine Longstaff and the Swiss guide Rudolph Aemmer, set out on the 25 mile trip to Assiniboine at the end of June, prior to the opening of the Alpine Club camp. Assisting Jimmy was Ernie Brearley, another English packer and guide, who was known affectionately as "Caruso" because of his fondness for singing on the trail. In his autobiography, *This My Voyage*, Longstaff later commented on the differences he noted on this trip between the Rockies and other mountain ranges of the world he was familiar with, saying he found the Rockies at once beautiful and haunting by their emptiness. However, he decided that for the mountain traveller they were ideal: "Beside clear streams are meadows of good pasture for horses and at each camp the axe supplies tent-poles for tepees, spring-mattresses of spruce and unlimited fuel. Nowhere is life in camp so delightful as in the Rocky Mountains."

The party made its approach by the normal route over Simpson Pass, allowing three days for the delights of camping, and only once did they run into windfall where "all hands must turn to and cut a path for the packhorses, who graze contentedly while we sweat." During the trip, Longstaff found Jimmy's services to be of a high order, and in his book commented on some wilderness tricks Jimmy had taught him: "Jimmy was an ideal companion: utterly competent, utterly imperturbable, yet his varied turns of speech to refractory cayuses were a revelation to me. Up to every dodge, he showed me how to preserve flour by dipping the sacks in a stream to form a protective crust against the rain. From him, too, I learned the priceless secret of drying wet matches in my hair."

When they arrived at Assiniboine's base, it was apparent that the mountain was in bad shape, a fact confirmed by fellow Englishman Felix Wedgwood (of pottery fame), who had just been turned back despite having the assistance of two Swiss guides. Miss Longstaff therefore had to abandon the attempt, and the two men set out to attack the icy giant on their own. It turned out to be the most difficult climb Longstaff ever experienced; a route up the steep north-west face in bad conditions, a long traverse to descend, and a tramp in darkness back to camp — 21 hours in all. A few days later Miss Longstaff was rewarded for her patience when she participated in a climb of a smaller peak to the north, which her compatriots named Katharine in her honour. Later she was contacted by the Canadian Geographic Board and informed that the name could not be used as it had already been applied to a different feature in the Rockies, Katherine Lake near Dolomite Pass. Asked to recommend an alternative, she suggested Wedgwood Peak in recognition of Felix Wedgwood, whom she had met at Assiniboine's base, came to know later at the Alpine Club camp and married soon after.

After their successes, Jimmy led the party out from Assiniboine by way of Bryant Creek, the Spray River and Whiteman's Pass. On their return they stopped for some fine trout fishing at one of his favourite spots on the Spray. Here he improvised a fishing pole for Miss Longstaff, made of a spruce limb with a string on it, weighted down with a bullet from his revolver and baited with a hook and bacon rind. With it she spent two happy days catching more fish than she had ever thought imaginable. At this camp the gentlemen ran out of tobacco and Jimmy again showed his skills at improvisation. He picked the leaves of a "rhododendron" and placed them by the fire until they were dry, then rubbed them gently until they crumbled into what all found to be a passably fine smoking substance. Miss Longstaff found him to be a wonderful even-tempered guide and she was particularly impressed by his skills with an axe: "To see him standing on a log wielding his axe was wonderful. Never a stroke too many, every stroke told, and the tree seemed to fall into its proper pieces at once."

On completion of the expedition, both Simpson and the Longstaffs repaired to the Alpine Club camp, the former to work and the latter two to enjoy a week's outing as the club's guests. In his book, Longstaff very succinctly summed up why these camps had gained such popularity and why they were so important for outfitters like Jimmy:

The system of Club meets was due to Wheeler's drive and enterprise. Apart from the social amenities and training value for young climbers, these camps formed a very practical solution of the chief problem of travel in the Rockies — expense. In the Himalaya, living off the country, I spent about £15 a month: in Canada the cost of a "pack train" was never less than £5 a day. A country uninhabited save for a few trappers and prospectors offers no resources: everything for a trip must be carried from start to finish and only very short forays can be made by back-packing. So for a mountaineering holiday on a moderate purse the ready-made headquarters of a standing camp with ample supplies is the only solution.

The main camp went of well under the Ottos' and Jimmy's care, but Wheeler was most unhappy with the subsidiary camp, which was provided with transportation by the Brewster company. This unforseen circumstance had occurred because the Ottos were in the process of selling out their business to the Brewsters prepatory to a move to the new country being opened up in the region of the Grand Trunk Pacific Railway at Jasper. Of course, this left the Alpine Club field wide open for Jimmy, and he was to take full advantage of the situation for several years.

CHAPTER FOUR

The Winter Trail

While heading north for a rendezvous with Outram for an attempt on Mount Forbes in 1902, Dr. J. Norman Collie came down the Mistaya River and near its mouth discovered a log cabin belonging to "two young trappers from Banff, Ballard and Simpson." In his book, *Climbs and Explorations in the Canadian Rockies*, Collie described its appearance and pondered on the life of those who engaged in this occupation:

The interior, which smelt very fusty and damp, was filled with skins, horns, traps of all kinds and sizes — conspicuous among them being two bear-traps, cruel-looking instruments like gigantic rabbit-traps, and requiring a force of nearly 400 lbs. to open the jaws when closed — tools of various sorts, and other trappers' instruments... The sight of such a shack, or cabin, as this in the wilds of the backwoods brings vividly before one the kind of life led by the trapper or miner or prospector up country; and the grit and endurance that a man must have to enter upon it... And how great must be the courage of the hunter or trapper who, in the depth of winter, ventures forth alone for weeks or months together in the woods, pack and blanket on back, dependent largely on his gun or rifle for food, and with none near to succour in case he falls ill or meets with an accident.

Like others who made their livelihood on the trail, Jimmy could not depend soley on the income from his summer outfitting, guiding and packing activities. The season was short — the trails were not dry enough nor the snow sufficiently melted to take tourist or mountaineering parties out much before the end of June, and the last hunting party usually came in around the end of October. This left up to eight months of the year to be filled with some other occupation that would help to keep body and soul together until the grass greened up and the pack saddles were hauled out for another go. Some of the trailmen took to a town occupation over the winter months, but most, including Jimmy, preferred to find some way to continue working in the outdoors. Often this meant doing some prospecting around an interesting outcropping discovered during a trip the previous summer, and during his life Jimmy would certainly be involved in some prospective mining propositions. But during his early years in the Rockies, he was much more attracted to trapping, for it seemed to provide a more certain return for the time invested and gave him the freedom he craved to move around and see the country. And the country he knew better than any was that between the upper Bow Valley and Wilcox Pass, an area that provided ideal habitat for pine marten, lynx, fox and bear.

The year Jimmy began trapping is not known for certain but it was likely about 1899, as he often referred to spending one winter trapping in the Mount Assiniboine area before moving his focus to the north of his campsite at Bow Lake. The skills necessary to be a trapper were undoubtedly picked up from a variety of people along the way, for it was an occupation practised by many at the time. In 1896 he had accompanied Smith, the old trapper from Lake Louise, on a few outings and he sometimes mentioned two Swedes who trapped north of Lake Louise in the last years of the century. In fact, it was probably the Swedes who constructed some of the cabins he would use himself, for as late as 1930 he would mention that these "marvels of axemanship," constructed without nails and with the logs fitting as if they had been planed, still stood.

These early Swedish trappers used skis to travel their traplines. Perhaps influenced by them, Jimmy once attempted to do so himself, and made a pair of skis from white pine in the woods "with axe and drawknife, bent and dried before an open fire, waxed with four candles I hated to use." He found that they worked satisfactorily until he became snowblind and ran one into a stump, breaking off the tip, after which "for 15 miles, not being able to distinguish the dips in the snow, that broken blade would go straight down while I went straight ahead and down so often that I ought to have contracted water on the brain." Apart from this misadventure, Jimmy used the normal implements of the country — snowshoes — which had been the standard means of winter travel from early fur trade days. As a trapper, he found that travel through close-growing timber while setting and attending traps lent itself more to snowshoes than skis. He quickly mastered the rolling gait required to make good time over the snow-covered landscape, and became so swift that the Stoney Indians of the Kootenay Plains area gave him his name, "Nashan-esen," in tribute.

Jimmy did not make his own snowshoes, preferring to buy the ready-made "Hudson's Bay variety," but when the new ones broke, as they often did, he would modify them for use in the snow conditions of the Rockies. The original webbing was babiche — caribou hide — that was essentially designed for the dry snow conditions found in the far north. In the more southerly latitudes of the Canadian Rockies there were times when the snow became soft and clogged up under the heel, bagging the webbing until it broke under pressure. Jimmy would keep an old goat hide handy to repair the snowshoes when this happened. The hair and wool would be peeled off the goat skin, which he found to be much tougher than caribou. He would then cut it into strips much larger than babiche and string it so that the holes between the strips were large enough to take the first joint of the little finger. These larger holes allowed the snow to sift through more easily when walking and prevented some of the balling that slowed him down and broke the webbing.

Jimmy spent many winters trapping north of Lake Louise, but none were as memorable as his first two with Fred Ballard. Days on the trapline were often long and arduous and there was little to keep one's mind active, other than reading. Ballard, with his Michigan backwoods background, became an interesting study for Jimmy during those times when they found themselves together:

When Ballard and I were first trapping each of us took something for winter. He took a bottle of Hennessey's brandy, I took a book, Bulwyer Lytton's Last of the Barons. The brandy went first, the book lasted all winter.

Ballard eventually read it. While he was reading it he got all worked up when he came to the part where Warwick, the King maker and King Edward got armies together and fought. I still remember the passage where Warwick was cracking the heads of the yokels to get there quick when Ballard made the same page and that ended it. He jumped up in a rage and cried "I wish I had been there with my Winchester; I would have made Warwick hump himself." I burst out laughing. A Winchester rifle would have been an innovation in those days. Ballard reached for the brandy bottle, looked at it sadly and asked as if it was my fault "Why do Hennessey have to use a bottle with the arse kicked in?" He was thinking that had the bottle been flat it would have held more liquid.

Ballard's rather bizzare way of dealing with things that bothered him extended beyond books and bottles to some of the equipment he used in trapping. Jimmy later recalled one time when he had to take cover when Fred's shoepacks acted up:

I remember snowshoeing up to timber line on Mt. Sarbach to see if there were any marten there. These animals have a habit of disappearing at times but that is because they are off looking for rabbits, their principal food in winter. Coming down we were wearing oil tanned shoepacks and the day was warm and little snow. Shoepacks in such weather are slippery as a cable of banana skins over a cavern in hell. We put the snowshoes under our arms and footed it coming down. On one steep grade which had snow on it I slid down on both feet. He followed my tracks instead of making one for himself. Half way down a piece of pine pole lying up and down hill caught in his instep, the end was rooted in the ground so he took a header into a log-jam at the bottom. The language was terrible so I hurried on to the cabin. When he got in he said not a word but tore off his shoepacks, grabbed his rifle and jammed in a cartridge, pointed it at his footwear and yelled "Move once, just once, you sons of bitches." I ducked outside roaring with laughter and hid behind the woodpile but he cooled off and didn't blow his footwear to pieces.

Despite the interesting moments Fred provided, Jimmy was glad when spring came and the pair headed back to town. Both men had strong personalities and undoubtedly they were both eager to part company after many months of enduring each other's idiosyncrasies. At the end of the 1903 season, Jimmy recalled, they ran out of food except for a few prunes, which they polished off before leaving their cabin on the Saskatchewan for civilization:

The snow had all gone up to the north side of Bow Pass so it was easy walking to the old cabin there. I had got a touch of snow blindness just previously but it was passing over. We had no snow glasses those days but I got it by tramping the south side of Mt. Wilson looking for anything to shoot. However I got only a spruce grouse which we cooked and halved — sort of a great divide — and I could hear Fred chomping the bones to small pieces to get all there was to get out of it. The eighteen miles was soon made.

Ballard had been teasing me about a new suit of underwear that had been in the cabin all winter and as to how nice it was going to feel inside it when he got to it. I understood. When we arrived he got to it all right but the cabin had leaked and it was sopping wet inside so we built a big fire outside and made camp. Fred squeezed the water out of it and spread it out in front of the fire carefully while I cooked up what flour was there and made a small bannock, and it was small. When cooked I halved it and his half past his tonsils as fast as a cable going over to the old country for more money while I sat on a log and ate my half slowly. That was too much for Fred. Pretty soon he snapped "If there is anything I hate to see it is a man chawing on a piece of bread that I could swallow in two bites, especially when he has only one good eye to chaw with." I understood.

We lay down to sleep before the fire but in the middle of the night I was awakened by bad language in time to see Ballard holding up a strip of his underwear with five button holes on it. A piece of charcoal had got to it while he was asleep so I thought consolations were due. "That's not too bad, " I said, "all it wants is new arms and legs and a piece on the back to fold over the chest, those five button holes are still quite good." The air was blue.

Undoubtedly because of his two years' experience trapping with Ballard, Jimmy's remaining career as a trapper was essentially a solo one. However, sometimes he would scout out some new territory with one of his compatriots to assist in laying out a new trapline. On one occasion he accompanied Bill Peyto on such a trip and had an unusual and somewhat harrowing experience. The two had stopped for a smoke beside a huge dead spruce and Jimmy drove his axe into it. From inside, it emitted a sound like some decaying matter falling down, so he hit it again with the back of the axe. He was about to do so again when, to his astonishment, the log opened up and the head of a two-year-old grizzly poked through:

Nine foot five is my record standing jump and I made it backwards, turning in mid air, and started to show squirrels how to climb a tree. I measured that jump next day with a copy of "Tid-Bits" that sported a foot rule on the cover. When I made the top I looked back . There was Bill cussing a blue streak and kicking that bear's head back every time it poked its nose through. It had gone into hibernation and was in semi-comotose condition but it was fast waking up. Bill called to me, I dropped out of the blue like a dose of measles and we lit out for camp. Next day we gathered it in.

Jimmy would meet his share of grizzlies, but never in such close quarters as this one.

After 1903, Jimmy took over the trapline between Bow Lake and the head of the Alexandra, while Ballard went on to establish a new one with his brother Jack in the vicinity of Fortress Lake. The work, formerly done by two men, was hard, consisting of 20 dozen sets spread out over this tremendous stretch of territory. Jimmy had some 14 to 16 cabins, lean-tos and shelters to provide protection in this distance. Travelling between them on snowshoes checking the traps as he went was somewhat tedious, which gave for his active and creative mind to go to work. Snowshoe travel developed a certain rhythm in his body, and as this rhythm established itself Jimmy would compose music to go along with it. Similarly, he would dream up one-act plays complete with all the characters and lines as he travelled along. If a bird flew across in front of him or something else diverted his attention, he would lose the storyline, but once the rhythm of the snowshoes was re-established it would all come back to him. Normally, as soon as he got into camp and started cooking dinner he couldn't remember a thing.

Collie, in his remarks about trappers, commented on "the awful loneliness of their solitary vigils" but found to his amazement that "not a few of them find pleasure in doing so." Jimmy was among these, and for many years, particularly before he had a wife and family, he enjoyed the months alone in the outdoors. After the labours of the day, he found that his harmonica was his great solace. Every night after dinner he would sit by the fire if he was in one of his cabins or under a tree by his campfire if he was camped outside, and play for several hours. He knew all the old songs, "Men of Harlot," "Annie Laurie," and many marching songs, and sometimes he would even try some operatic thing, improvising on his instrument to get the half notes. When the thermometer dipped to 40 below and he was in one of the cabins, he would step outside for a few minutes and play a bit to hear the sound travel in the cold air. This would get his dog Dooley to howling and soon there would be answering howls from every coyote for miles around, creating a real wilderness symphony.

On one occasion, Jimmy claimed that the symphony took on a different and much more realistic tone. It occurred early in 1904 at a cabin near the foot of the Lyell Glacier at the head of the Alexandra River. It had been a warm day and the evening was beautiful and clear when he stepped outside to admire the full moon. Off to the southwest, over Mount Lyell, he began to hear symphony music played by violins in a tune he did not recognize. The sound approached slowly, getting louder as it came nearer, and it passed over his head in an arc before moving off to the northeast and fading away. It was absolutely beautiful music, something he had never heard before and would never hear again, and he was convinced that he was not imagining or dreaming it. He did not mention this experience very often in later life, believing people would claim he was just bushed, but he found it to be "so genuine as to be almost frightening."

Jimmy knew the difference between a real experience and being bushed, for the latter also happened to him on more than one occasion when he had been out too long by himself. The incident he remembered best happened toward the end of one March when he was beginning to run a bit low on grub:

Fresh meat was about gone and through the glasses I had seen a large, dark mountain sheep high above timberline. This was on the west slope of Mount Wilcox. After breakfast I made sure of his location, and placed my snowshoes and rifle outside the cabin before dousing the fire. Your axe is always outside when you are away in case of fire. Without an axe you have a tough break. I snowshoed two miles up the gravel flats and before starting to climb took another look through the glasses. It was then I discovered I was carrying the axe and not the rifle and about then I said "James, it's about time you go and find someone else to talk to," and I did.

The state of mind the trapper's life could engender was not its only challenge, for there was also the very real threat to life and limb that went with it. As related, Jimmy's return from his Christmas visit to Tom Wilson's cabin on the Kootenay Plains provided the closest brushes with death that he had ever experienced. But they were not the only ones. On another occasion, he was travelling down a creek where light snow covered the ice, his snowshoes under his arm, when he stepped into a crack and pitched forward. He heard something crack, felt a dull pain in his shin, and had to scramble on his knees to reach for his rifle, which had slid toward some open water. His mind filled with dread while he carefully tested the leg, fearing that it was broken, but to his relief he found it was only wrenched and concluded that the cracking sound had likely been the ice breaking. It was a close call and Jimmy, with the fatalism typical of one surviving in the wilderness alone, accurately described what would have happened if it had been otherwise: "A broken leg 100 miles from the nearest habitation, an 8,000 foot pass and four feet of snow for the entire distance could mean but one thing. Load your rifle then look down the barrel to see if it is clean. Yes, that will be all!"

Hunting for game to help expand the winter's larder was another somewhat risky business in snowy conditions. Jimmy claimed that he never experienced real fear in his entire lifetime, but that one event had left him a little jittery. He had been hunting in the Brazeau River area in the winter and had managed to kill a sheep. After cutting the head off, he went to throw it over a cliff but it caught in the snow at the edge.

Without thinking much about it, he took off his snowshoes and slid on his behind down to where the head had become lodged and reached for it. All of a sudden, the snow around him gave way and went crashing over the 40 foot cliff. As it went, Jimmy was left suspended on the only slab that had remained, and he sat there thinking, "Is the rest going to come down and take me over?" Not daring to breath, he waited for the inevitable. When it didn't come, he slowly and gingerly inched his way back up the slope and got away, never stopping to see if the rest of the snow went over or not.

While serious injury meant almost certain death miles from assistance, Jimmy realized that there were other people trapping in the country who might provide help if he were only injured. Fortunately, he never had to rely on them, but he did assist others occasionally. One incident that stood out in his mind, requiring the toughest trip he ever knew one individual to make, involved his friend and former packer Sid Unwin:

He was trapping the Pipestone and Siffleur valleys, the Saskatchewan, Bear Creek and the Bow valley, a round trip of about 110 miles. He slept out the first half of the trip, but had shelters the rest of the way. By the Pipestone and Siffleur, the Saskatchewan is about 55 miles and due to snow conditions it took Unwin ten days to make this distance, eight of which was used in the first 25 miles.

Most people would have returned to Lake Louise until conditions became more favorable, but Unwin was one that having made up his mind to do a thing only death would stop him. On the head of the Siffleur, sleeping before an open fire he was so dog tired that he did not wake up until his mackinaw pants and underwear had burned to his flesh. Even then he snowshoed down to the Wilson ranch without a layover.

Tom told me that when he arrived at his ranch he had a bite to eat, answered vaguely a few questions, rolled back into an empty bunk and slept for 26 hours. When he joined me at the mouth of Bear creek a week later, the cloth of the cut away undergarment was still attached to him in a piece as large as the palm of the hand. Every day I would, as the burn healed, cut a piece of this away and his language, at times when I got too ambitious, made the operation a real pleasure. Antiseptics? No, just plain out of doors.

For the most part, trappers supported one another despite the fact that they were sometimes competing for the same animals. However, not everyone played by the rules, and those who did not were regarded as pariahs by Jimmy and his compatriots. A traveller visiting one of Jimmy's trapping cabins read a poem pencilled on the door "dedicated" to an offender who had been breaking in and stealing his grub:

These few lines are dedicated to the low-lived sucker who is in the habit of breaking in here.

*If you look for excitement, by ye here
When the owner hereof is standing near.
Proceed at the game of breaking in;
But mutter farewell to all your kin.*

*You son of a gun(?), you've not the nerve
To let the owner of this observe
The way in which the deed is done;
Or, J— C—, we'd have some fun.*

The height of Jimmy's trapping activities was in the years of the first decade of the century. By around 1910 he began to tire of spending the entire winter engaged in this solitary pursuit. While virtually all the profits from trapping were free and clear, and very little investment in equipment and food was required, the returns were not large. At best, a trapper could make six to eight hundred dollars in a season, but that was only if he was lucky and fur-bearing animals were abundant. Therefore, while he by no means gave up the trapline entirely, Jimmy began to look in other directions for a winter livelihood. He found one in a business that fit in very well with the growing popularity of his summer outfitting and guiding activity and its need for additional horseflesh.

In the years after the sale of his outfitting interests to Bob Campbell in 1904, Tom Wilson had spent much of his time raising horses and trading with the Stoney Indians at the ranch he had established on the south side of the North Saskatchewan River at Kootenay Plains. The prairie-like conditions and open winter ranges had proven agreeable to the livestock and Wilson's herd had increased accordingly. As well, in 1908 he had purchased the stock, buildings and interests of Elliott Barnes, another short-lived Banff outfitter and guide who had established a ranch on the plains across the river from Wilson in 1905. Although he tried to obtain government leases on both of these ranges, Wilson did not have much luck. This was followed by an even more unfortunate occurrence when he fell victim to frosbite while snowshoeing from the ranch to be with his family at Christmas in 1908. Due to a long convalescence, he had turned over most of the responsibility for the ranches to his eldest son, John Wilson. By 1911, Tom had begun to try to capitalize on his investment and agreed to sell Jimmy half of his interest.

Jimmy's original ten-horse pack string had probably grown slightly by the time he began discussing the Kootenay Plains deal with Wilson. The agreement would bring him half of the 140 head of horses on the Plains, placing him in an extremely strong position to compete with the larger outfitting interests, like Brewster's, as well as providing him with the wherewithal to become an important horse dealer. It would also give him a half interest in the buildings on the Plains and the leases on the range, if they could ever be gained. In return, he agreed to pay Wilson $2,000 immediately and another $2,000 when mutually agreed upon. The deal was completed on October 5, 1911 and shortly thereafter Tom Wilson officially turned over his remaining half interest in the livestock and ranches to his son John. Although the terms of this arrangement are not known, it appears from subsequent events that the elder Wilson still retained a legal interest. Shortly thereafter, on December 16th, Jimmy and John Wilson entered into a partnership agreement as "Wilson and Simpson" to run the ranches, with each putting in his half share of livestock and improvements. By its terms, the partners agreed to share equally in the expenses and profits of the operation, but the amount of money to be drawn out of the enterprise on an annual basis was to be limited to $500 each.

With his new investment and responsibilities, Jimmy's winter schedule changed accordingly. The horses spread out over the range had to be watched constantly to protect them from predators and to prevent them from wandering too far eastward into heavily forested land, where they would be difficult to find. As well, Jimmy and John Wilson intended to keep up the small trading activities that Tom Wilson had been carrying on with the Stoney Indians who frequented the Plains. When the season's outfitting and guiding activities were completed in the late fall, the pack train would be loaded up with trade goods and food and headed out over Pipestone Pass, down the Red Deer River and over the Siffleur onto the Plains. From that time forward, one or the other of the partners, if not both, would be constantly at the ranch over the winter months, their sojourns broken up by trips back and forth to Banff on snowshoes and by some trapping.

Winters at the ranch did not provide as many physical challenges as did the daily routine of running the trapline, but they were not without their moments. In one instance, Jimmy had to bring in a 14-horse pack train of goods and supplies on his own because he could not find any help. Heading up the Pipestone he ran into a severe fall blizzard and had to try to keep the horses from turning back, at the same time as trying to keep them on course in the obliterated landscape. Luckily, none of the packs fell off, because if they had in such conditions he could not have gotten off his horse to do anything about it. The ranch was eventually made, but Jimmy came near to freezing to death in the process.

Predators were also a problem sometimes, particularly when their normal food was scarce. Wolves were the most dangerous, and on one occasion Jimmy had a real scare when tracking a particularly large one. He had seen a huge black male hanging around the cabin and he put out some poison bait to try to dispose of him. Tracks in a fresh snow showed that the animal had visited the bait during the night, but he couldn't tell if any had been eaten. Jimmy threw on his snowshoes, grabbed his rifle and took off in hot pursuit, tracking the wolf through the snow. Travelling fast in the deep powder was tiring and it dulled his instincts, leading to a potentially dangerous mistake. As he came upon a small draw near the river into which the tracks led, he jumped into it without stopping to look. In a heart-stopping moment while in mid-air, he caught a glimpse of the wolf at the bottom of the draw, and he landed virtually on top of it. It was dead, having devoured some of the poison bait, but were it otherwise the animal might soon have been skinning Jimmy rather than vice-versa. The large black hide became a prize possession that adorned his home in Banff and provided an object for true-to-life tale telling.

The change in his winter schedule allowed Jimmy some time in town during the winter months after 1910. Always athletic, he became interested in two winter sports that would become part of his annual winter ritual for his entire life — hockey and curling. He had begun playing a bit of hockey on the river with some of the other young men of the town soon after his arrival in Banff. After a time he became more interested in coaching and developing the local boys than playing himself, and he organized several successful teams. For a couple of years around 1912 his teams won the provincial midget championships. As for curling, he was always an active participant, both as a player and as a volunteer taking care of the local curling ice. Until it was destroyed in a fire at Cochrane, a trophy he put up, the Simpson Cup, was one of the most hotly contested championships in the Bow Valley. In later years, Jimmy recalled his introduction to the roaring Game:

The first big bonspeil I remember in Banff took place soon after I joined the club — around 1910 I think. There was curling on the ice in front of Dr. Brett's place, where the Administration Building is now, and the rink was very handy to the bar. As the day went on the match was taken less and less seriously . . .

I remember at one point we heard a fearful uproar coming from the hospital section of Dr. Brett's place. . . The doctor dashed up the stairs followed by some of the curlers. Upstairs in the hospital there was a long polished corridor running the length of the building. As we approached we could hear the cries of "Centre ice, old chap! Don't be short" — followed by hideous crashes. In the corridor were three well known re-mittance men holding a bonspeil of their own with crockery collected from under the beds.

"Yes," Jimmy thought, "Banff is definitely beginning to grow on me."

CHAPTER FIVE

The Hunter's Art

The purchase of half of Wilson's interests and livestock at the Kootenay Plains gave Jimmy a tremendous boost in the guiding and outfitting business. While he had done well outfitting tourist and mountaineering parties and working for organizations such as the Dominion Topographic Survey and the Alpine Club of Canada in the summer months, he now needed to expand his fall business to survive in the face of strong competition. The most successful outfitters were those noted for their skill as hunting guides as much as for their trail abilities, and at the end of the century's first decade Jimmy was well on his way to establishing such a reputation.

His proficiency as a hunter had improved markedly since his first forays into the mountains when he had almost blown his head off. Working for Wilson as a cook on numerous hunting parties had provided him with the rudiments, but it was really his years on the trapline that provided the fine tuning of the basics he had learned. Hunting was critical to keeping the larder stocked during the winter months and for some species, like bear, spring shooting provided a valuable supplement to the marten and fox pelts taken from the traps. But it was the opportunity the trapline allowed for observation that was to be its greatest value. Jimmy was, and would remain for his entire life, a keen observor of nature. Weeks and months spent on the trapline over a period of years encompassing a broad expanse of territory gave him the opportunity to learn the favourite haunts of each species of animal, its habits, its daily and seasonal patterns of movement, and its preferred food. In addition, when he began to spend part of each year on the Kootenay Plains, he became friends with the Stoney Indians who frequented the area, and, as their livelihoods depended on it, many of them were renowned hunters. After quickly picking up the basics of the Stoney language, he often conversed with such noted stalkers as Jonas Benjamin and Sampson Beaver, and occasionally hunted with them.

Few of the other guides along the CPR trapped as assiduously as Jimmy did, they did not have the advantages provided by his ranch, nor were they as observant as he, so it was not surprising that he quickly became one of the leading hunting guides in the area. But it went even deeper — Jimmy was the kind of man who was not content to sit back and let the world come to him, he went out after it. So it was with his hunting business. A contact he made in 1910 became the key to unlocking a treasure-trove of wealthy American sportsmen anxious to experience the wilderness and beauty of the Rockies while they sought trophy heads of sheep, goat, moose and bear to adorn the walls of their offices and dens. He offered to take that contact out hunting for free, providing he would turn his considerable artistic skills to depicting the animal that Jimmy regarded as the finest to be found in his territory, the bighorn sheep. It was to be the beginning of a lifelong friendship with North America's foremost big game artist, Carl Rungius.

The German-born Rungius, almost a decade Jimmy's senior, had received his basic art training in Europe before arriving to visit an uncle in New York for a moose hunt in 1894. The hunt proved unsuccessful, but the young painter was so taken with the New World that he emigrated permanently to the United States the following year. A chance meeting with a Wyoming guide at the Sportsmens' Show in Madison Square Gardens had led to several visits to the American west in the late 1890s, allowing him to hone his considerable drawing skills on specimens of antelope and elk he was able to shoot. At the same time, during winters spent in New York, he came to the attention of Dr. William T. Hornaday, director of the New York Zoological Society's Bronx Zoo and a founding member of the Boone and Crockett Club, an organization limited to 100 of America's leading sportsmen and conservationists. Hornaday was to become Rungius's mentor, gaining him charter membership in another important outdoorsman's club, the Campfire Club of America, and providing him with wealthy contacts to purchase his growing and improving body of wildlife art. He also arranged for Rungius to accompany a biological expedition to the

Yukon Territory in 1904, under the leadership of Charles Sheldon, to investigate the type of mountain sheep that inhabited those northern latitudes. It was this trip that was to provide, inadvertently and circuitously, the source of his lifelong association with the Canadian Rockies and his friendship with Jimmy.

When he returned from the Yukon, Rungius painted one of his most dramatic pieces, six white Dall sheep on a high mountain ridge. *Wary Game* took Hornaday's fancy and he had it reproduced in the January, 1910 issue of the *Bulletin* of the New York Zoological Society. Sometime previously Jimmy, interested in information about animals and probably hoping to live trap and sell sheep and goats to the Bronx Zoo, had become a member of the Society. On one of his infrequent visits home from the trapline, he picked up the *Bulletin* with his mail and began leafing through it. He possessed a keen eye for art, and was struck by the reproduction of Rungius's painting, both because of its subject matter and because of the professional way in which it had been portrayed. With typical zeal, he immediately sat down a wrote a letter to Rungius, care of the Society, indicating his admiration for the artist's work and offering him his services for free if he would come to the Rockies and paint bighorns. A skeptical Rungius read the letter and then crumpled it up and threw it away, muttering to his wife Louise that it was just another guide looking for another client. Her interest piqued, she pulled it out of the trash, read it, and, detecting the fine hand of an educated man, convinced her husband that it was a serious offer that should be accepted. This resulted in a flurry of correspondence that ended in August, 1910 with the Rungiuses bound from New York for the Canadian Rockies on a CPR pass arranged by Jimmy.

Upon arrival, Rungius wasn't sure that his original opinion hadn't been correct, for Simpson was not there to meet them as he had said he would be. After finding a hotel, he dumped all his equipment and went off in search of the missing guide. Rungius found him at home, and Jimmy explained that the train had come in on time, a most unusual occurrence, and that he had arrived at the station platform just after the Rungiuses had departed. On laying eyes on each other they both had a good laugh, for they realized that they had actually seen each other passing on the station road. Jimmy had expected a bigger man than the slight but tough painter, while Rungius had expected a strapping Canadian woodsman rather than the wiry, red-haired guide.

Jimmy was intending to take Rungius to his favourite sheep-hunting haunt, the Brazeau River basin, which lay to the north and east of the Columbia Icefield. He had first visited this area in about 1908, acting on information given to him by the Indians at Kootenay Plains, and it soon became the northern limit of his trapline. It provided exactly the right mix of habitat and high valleys favoured by the sheep, and was also outside the recently extended boundaries of Rocky Mountains Park. In 1902 the federal government, reacting to calls for better protection of the Rockies' game population and the incorporation of more lands into the original 260 square mile park around Banff townsite, expanded the park to 4,400 square miles. Its northern boundary then reached to encompass all of the headwaters of the Bow River and part of those of the North Saskatchewan, and within these boundaries hunting was illegal. Because the boundary was not actually demarcated on the ground and there was as yet no organized warden service to enforce the regulations, Jimmy did not pay particular attention to this restriction in his personal hunting activities. However, the parks branch had indicated that it was serious by instituting a guides' licensing system and a register of pack train parties in 1909, and when he had a party out with him Jimmy realized that it was best to hunt outside the boundary whenever possible. This made the territory north of the main branch of the North Saskatchewan his usual objective.

After Rungius had spent a week or so sketching in the Ptarmigan Valley region near Laggan, the pack train set out for the north in late August with Jimmy as guide and Ernie Brearley assisting as cook and packer. The usual two days travel brought them to Jimmy's favourite campground at Bow Lake and after crossing Bow Pass the next day, despite the fact that they were still in the park, they began to hunt in earnest. Near Upper Waterfowl Lake some goats were spotted high up on Pyramid Peak (Mount Chephren) and, as he had never seen this species before, Rungius was determined to get one. A climb through some timber brought them to the valley where they had spotted the animals and, although most of them had moved off, one lone billy remained and the artist easily bagged it. His success required a delay that would not normally occur with a hunting party, but one Jimmy would soon get used to when out with Rungius — a day's layover so the artist could immediately do some pencil drawing field sketches of the animal he had just taken. Jimmy marvelled at Rungius' method of ensuring as accurate a reproduction as possible, which involved stuffing the goat's gutted carcass with grass and branches and then stringing it up with a tripod and ropes to approximate its pose in the wild.

Proceeding across the North Saskatchewan, the horses were turned up the gravel flats of the North Fork all the way to its head, and a brief visit to Wilcox Pass was made to show the artist the glories of Mount Athabasca and the Columbia Icefield. Then it was back down to Nigel Creek and over Nigel Pass toward the headwaters of the Brazeau River. Jimmy knew a shortcut into the Brazeau basin by way of Jonas Pass, and as they neared it Carl spotted a grizzly bear about a mile away. The encounter was to give Rungius the opportunity to observe one of those freak occurrences in nature that very few of the outfitter's clients were ever lucky enough to witness:

On the way up we noticed fresh bear sign and reaching the top of the pass I saw a large grizzly just disappearing behind a little hill about a mile ahead. The outfit halted and Simpson said, 'Get busy!' Jerking the rifle from my saddle started in the direction of the bear.

When I reached the general locality I saw a gopher sitting up on top of a little hill, intently watching something on the other side. From this I knew that the bear was near. But I was not prepared for what followed.

I stalked carefully up the hill, when suddenly a black fox rose up directly in front of me; he was stalking the gopher! The black fox is always a rarity, in the wild state, and this was a beautiful animal, so the temptation to take him was great. But I wanted the bear, so I passed up the fox. When I reached the top there was the grizzly, walking broadside to me, not over 50 feet away.

My shot through the shoulder paralyzed him, he fell with his back in a hole he had been digging and never rose again, but sat upright grabbing his hind legs with his front paws and biting at them. Jim said that he could hear the bear roaring; but I was so intent on getting the grizzly that I never noticed it. I finished off the animal and my outfit came up and afforded us with an amusing incident.

The "amusing incident" Rungius referred to was the sight of packer Ernie Brearley jumping on the dead grizzly, pulling out a bottle and poking through the animal's hide, "working as thoroughly as a monkey" to find fleas. When one was discovered it was popped into the bottle and hoarded "as carefully as though they were flakes of gold," as he had a standing order from a British collector at twenty cents per flea. Although this particular collection was somewhat unusual, trailmen often tried to supplement their income by collecting specimens of one type or another. Jimmy himself corresponded with numerous scientists, bird collectors and seekers of the rare who asked him to collect everything from eggs to flowers to skins, and offered him good prices for his finds.

After Rungius completed the obligatory sketches, the party proceeded on its way to the Brazeau. Although game proved rather scarce in the region that year, Rungius was fortunate enough to get one small ram, which he sketched and painted with enthusiasm, and when he returned to Banff to meet his wife a short time later he pronounced himself well pleased with the results of the trip. While he had been successful in bagging some useful subject matter, the game he had taken was not particularly large and he had missed an opportunity to get a really good goat on the North Saskatchewan because of a bad case of buck fever. The incident was recorded by Jimmy in a humourous little piece he wrote for Rungius under the title "Goat or Hoodoo?" in two acts. Act I occurred in 1910:

"Py shingo, if dat dem set trigger hadn't been froze up, dat billy would be dead. Sure. Dat is too bad. He vas a granddad villiam & stood dare on legs four feet high. Dem it, it's no shoke."

So said my artist friend as we sat on a high ridge of 10,000 ft. altitude on the North Saskatchewan & looked sadly at a large rock jutting behind which a huge Rocky Mountain goat had vanished on a slow lope. . . .

It was a long hard grind to get within range, & I believe we could have gotten within fifty yards, but unfortunately the melting snow made

*footing treacherous & noisy, & when some 150 yards away he deliber-
ately looked us over, rose to his feet, turned & walked away. As he did
so he turned scornfully & looked us over most insultingly.*

*"I'll try him," said my friend as he jammed a cartridge with a rattle
like a threshing machine, pressed the set trigger & aimed. Click, nothing
doing, set trigger froze up, & "Dem it, vat de hell's de matter?" from my
right.*

*After that, bang. The goat stopped & looked back mildly surprised.
Bang, bang, bang. He hastened a trifle & gained a pile of snow-covered
rocks & looked at us. Bang, bang, click. Magazine empty & "Dem it," as
another clip was being rammed into the magazine.*

*Billy evidently thought something was on for he hastened somewhat,
& as he took to a snowslope in open sight of us, bang, bang, again. The
last bullet ploughed up the snow just above him and he headed directly
across our front. Bang, bang, bang, click. "Vat's the matter" from my
right again.*

*Bang. The bullet ploughed a hole in the snow between the goat's hind
legs. Bang, just over his head, then "Py shingo, he's gone," from my right
again.*

*Perhaps I laughed. I suppose I must have done to occasion the remarks
in the beginning. I know I did when he mournfully exclaimed, "Dat is
the limit. Thirteen cartridges vasted & dat dem goat going yet. If dat dem
set trigger —" Yes, I know I laughed.*

The second act of the farce documented Rungius' further pursuits of the
same goat the following year, with the same result. Although probably
written only to entertain his new friend, the story illustrated Jimmy's
facility for writing, something he had not tried previously. As the years
went by he would begin to do more in his spare time, eventually finding
a ready audience in the outdoor magazine market.

Over the course of the following winter, Rungius began to turn his
sketch material into paintings, including one featuring the bear entitled
An Old Prospector, wherein the impressive mountain landscape was
given equal importance with the animal itself. This marked the beginning of a new development in his painting, an appreciation of the
intrinsic value of landscape, and Rungius expanded on it the next year

when Jimmy took him back to the same territory. This time he brought a friend, fellow artist Philip Goodwin, who had a studio near his in New York and had a reputation as the best outdoor illustrator of the day. Since Goodwin had never hunted in the west, Jimmy and Rungius instructed him in hunting techniques as best they could, hammering home the golden rule that he should never go out painting without a rifle. Taking the education to heart, Goodwin went out sketching and painting time after time with gun in hand, but never saw a thing. Then one day he forgot to carry it and while he was painting on a narrow ledge above a river a large grizzly appeared only 40 feet away. Bear and painter were equally surprised at the meeting and it seemed to Goodwin that they stood facing each other for an eternity before the grizzly suddenly swung around and jumped into the river.

Goodwin greatly enjoyed the opportunity that Jimmy's hospitality afforded him and wrote to thank him in December, 1911. In his letter he commented, "This year's trip, all in all, has been the best ever and I sure appreciated what you and Carl have done in making such a trip possible for me." Jimmy kept the letter and had it framed, for on the front of it was a typical Goodwin illustration — Rungius standing in front of Jimmy holding a smoking rifle while his "Hoodoo" goat gazed impassively at them from a near-by mountain-side. Goodwin entitled it "A Picture Without Words."

Jimmy's admiration for Rungius' art soon became boundless, for in it he saw the embodiment of the mountain landscape, atmosphere and wildlife that he so loved. When Jimmy expressed an interest in learning a bit about painting himself, Rungius tried to help, and the two jointly painted a sheep in a mountain setting in 1911. More often he preferred just to observe while a picture took shape on Rungius' easel in the field. Sometimes he would tease the artist by asking, "What have you got there, Carl?" as Rungius reached for another tube of paint to put in a sky, and then following it up with, "I'd a damn sight sooner have your palette than that." But a few minutes later he'd look again and exclaim, "Jesus, Carl, that's a beautiful thing!" On one occasion Rungius started to draw his saddle horse and as Jimmy looked over his shoulder he said: "My God, that's my saddle horse — its absolutely perfect. That looks to me like Remington at his best." "Well, it's a long way from Remington," responded Rungius. "Yes," Jimmy retorted, "you're alive and he's dead." A similar bolstering of the artist's confidence would take place when Carl complained that he wasn't getting enough money for his paintings, at which point Jimmy would impatiently tell him it was because "you don't think you're as good as you are."

During Rungius' first two visits to the Rockies, Jimmy provided him with all his outfit and guide services as well as the hospitality of his own home. But he could not afford to do so indefinitely, nor did the artist require the assistance of a guide after learning his way around, for he had often guided himself during his days in Wyoming. Therefore, over the next few years, the two worked out a most interesting and mutually satisfactory agreement — Jimmy supplied Carl with a few pack horses and one of his men to assist with packing and cooking for an annual hunting and painting trip and in return Rungius gave him a painting. Through this arrangement, Jimmy acquired nine major pieces exhibiting the animals, landscape and activities that his lifestyle embodied. Eventually they would become extremely valuable but for the time being they simply helped to satisfy Jimmy's growing collecting habit, a habit which would lead to the amassing of one of western Canada's finest wildlife art collections.

Rungius' trade of paintings for pack horses was not the only valuable consideration that Jimmy gained from their strengthening relationship. The artist's stature with members of the Campfire Club and other wealthy eastern American sportsmen eager to procure his paintings led to several important connections for Jimmy with those anxious to experience a hunt in the territory where Rungius gathered his material. In fact, Rungius paintings became one of Jimmy's most effective advertisements. Apart from painting, Rungius also took photographs in the field, and after returning to New York he would have some of them made into prints and lantern slides to show to his friends and acquaintances in the outdoor world.

As early as 1912, Dr. Hornaday himself was in correspondence with Jimmy to ask for information on bighorn sheep for a book he was writing on the Rockies. This was followed by a request to capture some goat kids and a mountain sheep ram for inclusion in the Bronx Zoo, the offer being for $500 plus $150 for expenses to care for them on their way to New York. Although Jimmy tried, he soon became too busy to spend much time on this exercise, as by 1912 the first of several subsequently important sportsmen clients began to appear at Banff. Key among them was Dr. Harlow Brooks, one of New York's most famous diagnosticians and a man who had hunted widely. Jimmy took him out in 1912, and in 1915 he returned with a group of fellow Campfire Club members. Brooks' friends had hunted together often, usually with hunting guide Joe Jones of Valley, Wyoming, Jimmy's foremost competitor south of the line. Apart from Brooks, the main participants were John Murgatroyd, a New York businessman, and Joe McAleenan, a diamond dealer and appraiser for Tiffany's who at one time owned the Hope Diamond. Because they had hunted so frequently, Murgatroyd and McAleenan intended to do most of their hunting with the camera so that "trophies could be carried home on film and plate, and the glad, strong, wild creatures still left to roam their beloved hills and peaks, and enjoy their right to life and happiness." Brooks, on the other hand, was intent on bagging a bighorn sheep and, above all, a grizzly bear. Two other friends, Ambrose Means and E. R. Sanborn, came along to capture the trip on an early version of the motion picture camera.

When the party arrived on the train from the east, they went directly to Jimmy's house to rest and freshen up. McAleenan, who recorded the trip in a diary that he subsequently had published in a hand-coloured limited edition of twenty, was as surprised as most of Jimmy's clients when he first entered the house, expecting the rude surroundings of the frontiersman:

The cottage shone white through a setting of pines. A little red squirrel chattered a shrill welcome to us as we approached the porch. Outside, the house differed little from its neighbors; the interior was its distinction.

An upright piano stood against the east wall. Pelts of bear, cat and wolf covered the floor and hung over comfortable chairs. There was the latest Victrola, with records of Caruso, Kubelik and other great artists. On the walls hung paintings of landscapes and animals, typical of the owner's taste. Here, appearing at their best, were the beautiful works of Carl Rungius, a friend of Simpson's, a splendid library of books, the titles of which paid an eloquent tribute to their owner. A great couch stretched invitingly across the fire-place. In the rough cement hearth cartridge shells were imbedded, souvenirs of many a hunting camp, spelling in big letters the word "Welcome." Such was the home we found far off in this quaint Canadian village.

I do not know why I was astonished, apart from the tendency of all humanity to decide for themselves the character and tastes of others without consulting that other, but astonished I was.

Here was a man whose days and years had been spent in the mountain wilderness, who knew from close association the life habits of its animals. Who had rubbed elbows with the roughest side of life. Yet here we found him, knowing and loving and living with the best of music, art and literature.

The next day the hunters made their way to Lake Louise where they joined Jimmy's pack train for the journey north. The Brazeau country was once again the objective and the first few days on the trail proved to be most enjoyable. McAleenan quickly grew to admire his guide and spent a good deal of his time finding out what made him tick. The evening campfire, the time of the day for camaraderie, tall tales and discussion, provided the best opportunity, and the two took full advantage of it. Noted McAleenan in his diary, "Jim Simpson and I sat up late into the night, telling our most choice lies, some True Stories, and winding up with philosophy on life — and Jim is SOME philosopher." This, he said, was understandable if one had "to go unflinching along the steep rough trails that Jim had walked."

Good weather and grand scenery accompanied the party as far as Nigel Pass but on September 1st the air turned cold and overnight a heavy rain turned to snow. It marked the beginning of two solid weeks of early winter weather in the high country that made travel over the passes difficult, if not dangerous, and caused havoc with the hunting and film-making. The fickle nature of mountain weather was something Jimmy always had to deal with in his guiding activities, but long, cold, snowy periods during the fall were particularly troublesome because the parties were usually farther from the railway and out for a longer time. He tried his best to keep spirits up during tedious days in camp when standing around a big fire was about the only activity possible, drawing on his vast repertoire of stories and conversing with his clients on subjects that were of interest to them. In fact, like Will Rogers, he made it a point to study up on his clients' interests before going out with them, so that he could discuss things intelligently during these slow periods. As he put it, "That way they wouldn't have to listen to me recite the first 87 stanzas of the cowboy's lament."

McAleenan's group had hunted often enough to be familiar with such circumstances and, diverted by the boyish humour and good-natured ribbing that went with men out on a hunting trip, they managed to keep their spirits up. Dr. Brooks, the great hunter, was often the butt of their antics, particularly after he shot a bear that the others decided was so small that it must have been a teddy bear bought in New York and smuggled out with the pack train. They decided to covene a court and try "Dr. S. B." for murder:

After dinner we gathered around the fire and court was convened to try Brooks for deliberate, premeditated and atrocious murder. John was the judge, and Means was Brooks' attorney. Simpson was called, and after a close vote was declared mentally responsible and able to serve as a competent witness.

Witness Simpson described the innocent Teddy Bear sitting on a rock near the river, and also dwelt upon Brooks' vicious excitement. He said the prisoner called out savagely, "Where is the bear?" "Right there, Doctor," said the witness.

"Where?" asked Brooks.

"Right over there — on the rock nearest the river."

"Did you bring your gun, Simpson? — mine might jam — where the h— is the bear?"

Witness further stated that old Seven Barks' rage was fearful. He leveled his rifle and shot the poor little Teddy Bear in the stomach. Teddy fell from the rock with one last grunt — for he had his grunting machinery located in his mid-riff.

The body of the deceased was exhibited and the defiant Brooks said, "To h— with you all."

Judge Murgatroyd charged the jury for a verdict of murder in the first degree. The jury so decided, without leaving their logs. Old Seven Barks was convicted of murder in the first degree, and sentenced to treat everybody who came into the King Edward Hotel for thirty minutes after our arrival.

Seven Barks said that there was a woman at the bottom of this plot to ruin his hunting reputation. That she hatched out this plot and purchased the bear in New York. He was led away.

Other means to pass the time were also created, including a giant snowball fight launched by Simpson, who was bombarded mercilessly until he had to sue for peace. But the more serious business of hunting was also pursued diligently when the weather allowed, and near the Brazeau Glacier Jimmy was able to find Dr. Brooks his sheep. It was a big old ram nearing the end of its days and its head, with a 22 inch spread and a 38½ inch curl, made just the trophy the doctor was seeking. A few other smaller sheep were also spotted, but McAleenan reported that overall game was very scarce, a factor attributed by Simpson to the depredations of poachers and the Stoney Indians. In the midst of these troubles one of Jimmy's guides, Ulysses LaCasse, arrived with another hunter he was outfitting, Heywood Cutting of Boston, who wasn't in a particularly good frame of mind. McAleenan wrote that Jimmy was going to spend a few days with him in a "forlorn-hope-hunt" and passed the observation that "Cutting has been unfortunate, and seems to feel that the guide and the country are at fault."

McAleenan's party headed back for Banff in mid-September under the care of Jimmy's cook Jim Boyce and packer Ben Woodworth, searching for goat to fill out the larder as they retreated. On the way, at Brazeau Lake, they ran into Tom Wilson, out for the Canadian Water Supply Survey, and later near Nigel Pass they discovered Carl Rungius out with one of Jimmy's men sketching and hunting. Near the North Saskatchewan River, Jimmy rejoined the party and after he had guided Murgatroyd on a full day's hunt on Mount Wilson they succeeded in getting a goat at dusk. This was followed by additional success on Mount Chephren, where four more billys fell to the hunters' guns, that area now being outside the park with the boundary change of 1911 taking it back to the headwaters of the Bow. In the final analysis, McAleenan was able to pronounce the trip a complete success despite the vagaries of the weather, and closed his diary with an insight on what an experience of this type meant to those involved: "Together we have wandered through the forests, crossed the muskeg, climbed passes and forded rivers. Together we have eaten the fare of the wilderness. Within sight of the mighty glaciers and ice fields we have pitched our tents and built our campfires. A brotherhood is born on these trips, stronger than the ties of blood, and everlasting." With feelings such as these being expressed, it is not surprising that this would not be the last time Jimmy would see McAleenan and company.

Of course, not all trips would end with such fine sentiments being expressed by the participants. In 1916 Robert Frothingham, another leading member of the Campfire Club, finally booked a hunting trip with Jimmy after three years of corresponding about it. Frothingham made his living as an outdoor writer and lecturer, touring the United States with lantern slides entertaining audiences with stories of his various expeditions and hunts. He therefore relied on his reputation as a great hunter and completely competent outdoorsman for his livelihood, but Jimmy found him to be somewhat lacking in shooting skills. He related that while out on the trail the great hunter experienced a bad case of buck fever and that "one day Frothingham nearly shot me through the back and the next day his hunting companion nearly shot me through the stomach." Such remarks eventually found their way back to New York and Frothingham took them as an insult, and he didn't hesitate to tell his fellow club members what he thought of his guide. Fortunately for Jimmy, the tempest eventually cooled and he came back into Frothingham's good graces, resulting in the publication of two hunting stories that complimented Jimmy highly on his abilities as a guide and his sterling qualities as a human being.

One of the things Frothingham wrote perhaps captured better than anything else Jimmy's feelings about hunting: "Simpson is, without doubt, the best hunter and most expert stalker of Bighorn Sheep in Western Canada. To quote his own words he would rather stalk sheep than occupy the front seat in the heavenly choir." Jimmy himself rarely spoke about his feelings on hunting, as it had become such an integral part of his existence. He essentially regarded game as a resource to be harvested and a means of staying in business. It was also a source of food for both the trail and at home in Banff during the long winter months, which accounted for his poaching activities. Usually these were carried on with relative impunity, as many mountain residents supplemented their larder with a bit of local game, but as the parks authorities became serious about enforcing regulations they kept a particularly close watch on him as a likely culprit. In late 1916, they caught him with the goods.

In December, 1916 Jimmy appeared in Banff court to answer charges on three offences: "With killing a mountain sheep three and a half miles west of Banff, along the motor road on or about Nov. 18; with unlawfully having portions of a mountain sheep in his possession; with having killed a mountain sheep near the 7 mile post on the motor road on or about Nov. 14." Jimmy defended himself, but the case against him seemed to be airtight. The offences had occurred along his wood limit adjacent to the motor road, the carcass of a sheep and a scalpless head had been found under separate log piles, and the next day wardens had searched his home and found the scalp of a sheep and a quantity of wild game meat in his attic. The wardens testified that the scalp of the sheep fit perfectly to the head they had discovered under the log pile. Despite the fact that "all the witnesses were severally cross-examined by Simpson" and he took the stand in his own self defense, the magistrate found him guilty on all three charges. As it was his first offense, the minimum fine, totalling $126, was imposed, and his guide's license was taken away.

Privately, Jimmy did not dispute the fact that he was guilty, but nevertheless he claimed that the wardens had perjured themselves to convict him. According to him, the scalp of the sheep taken from his attic did not fit the head of the sheep they had found because he had burned about eighteen inches of the skin in his furnace. The penalty was and expensive one, costing him the equivalent of more than a week's wages — he was charging a rate of $100 per week per person for outfitting and guiding services at the time — but the loss of his guide's license was potentially more serious. However, he cleverly found a way around the problem by making sure that one of his packers registered out as guide while he registered out as packer and then taking charge of the pack train as soon as it was outside the park boundary.

Jimmy's attitudes about hunting and poaching didn't mean he was not a conservationist or that he was unfeeling about taking the life of a wild animal. Like most of his clients, who were leaders in the conservation movement in the United States as well as avid hunters, he realized that measures to ensure healthy game populations were necessary to protect the animals he hunted. Like many guides and outfitters, his perception was that the greatest threat to game populations was overhunting by Indians, and he frequently spoke out about it in his conversations with government officials, seeing no contradiction in the fact of his own poaching activities. On the other hand, he sometimes went to great lengths to save young animals he felt were imperilled, Frothingham witnessing one such event on his trip. The hunters were pursuing goat in the Brazeau along a high cliff when they saw a young kid apparently go straight over. On peering over the edge, they saw that it had actually only gone a short way down and had become lodged in a cleft in the rock. Without hesitation, Jimmy climbed down at great risk to himself, dislodged the youngster and brought it back up to safety in his arms.

The closest that Jimmy ever came to expressing the innate tragedy associated with his occupation was in a short article he wrote on hunting entitled "Out On The Deep, Soft Snow:"

Have you wakened when the stars are paling and listened to the song of the white-crowned sparrow, who never seems to sleep? Have you watched the soft early light appear, felt the "pull" of the sleeping bag, the silence, the mystery and the joy of the new spring day? Have you watched the rose tints of the rising sun swell, turn paler; heard the song of the robin, the music of the brook; faint music during the frozen night but soon to swell to a sullen roar as the snows melt in the midday sun? Have you done this and not felt rather ashamed that your mission is one of death?
. . .

Visualize this: A clear cold morning in early May, with the first rays of the sun bursting on the higher peaks. Snow frozen hard enough to dispense with the snowshoes, but before long it will soften and travel for the day will be over. The sun peeps through a break in the ranges and floods the valley with a soft, warm light, but the open water of a clear spring creek calls a halt to look for a crossing, dry shod. A fallen log forms a bridge, but before it can be reached the willows part and a large grizzly walks into the open. He shakes himself and you see over the rifle sights the sheen of his long, silky coat. The wind is right and he has not seen you, but as the discharge echoes, and re-echoes it does not drown the savage roar of the stricken animal. He plunges head-long toward you unconscious of your presence, but of that you are not aware. Something tickles up and down your spine and your very hair roots fill with motion. You hear him splash in the open creek and stand, every muscle tense, awaiting his reappearance. It seems like hours — it is but seconds. Then you see him lying motionless in the clear cold water, a trailing line of crimson winding slowly past. Gingerly you approach, but there is not need for care, only strength, strength to pull the huge bulk to the gravel beach, where the final chapter may be written with the hunting knife. And through it all the robins sing and the chipmunks play, oblivious that another tragedy in their world of tragedies has happened.

The story ends with Jimmy musing on the meaning of the event, and he comes down firmly on the side of its worth to the one who has experienced it, perhaps summing up the appeal of hunting to his clients: "This is a fair sample of a spring bear hunt. It may sound hard. It is. It may sound foolish, but is it? It has its compensations and pleasures. Were life-giving health the sole reward it would be full or worth it, but the memories that will never fade are yours and yours alone."

Jimmy with his friend Dooley, ca. 1900

Jimmy sporting all the accoutrements of a trail guide, ca. 1905.

Jimmy quickly learned all the tricks of packing and tying the famous "diamond hitch"

*Jimmy adopted the stiff-brimmed "pony stetson" so it wouldn't blow
over his field glasses while spotting game*

*Fred Ballard at one of his and Jimmy's rough-hewn trapping cabins,
ca. 1903*

Jimmy assisting "the butterfly lady" in her collecting, ca. 1905

Jimmy preparing to pack baggage for the Vermilion Pass Alpine Club camp, 1912. F.V. Longstaff photograph

Jimmy guiding T.G. Longstaff through burnt timber on the way to Mount Assiniboine, 1910

Billie as photographed by Jimmy while visiting his home, ca. 1915

The Simpson family — Jimmy, Margaret, Mary, Billie — ca. 1919

Jimmy with Jimmy jr. in the saddle, 1926

Is Your State Wet or Dry? See the Prohibition Poll Returns

The Literary Digest

Vol. 105, No. 2
Whole No. 2086

April 12, 1930

Price 10 Cents

© Grand Central Art Galleries, New York   "THE MOUNTAINEER"—By Carl Rungius

*Carl Rungius sometimes used Jimmy as a model, as in this piece
entitled "The Mountaineer"*

CHAPTER SIX

A Guide in New York

During his first two decades in the Canadian Rockies, Jimmy had progressed from an unknown trail cook to one of the area's foremost "mountain men." His reputation as a peerless hunting guide, an ironman wilderness traveller, an equestrian and handler of horses of noteworthy skill, a self-trained naturalist and a "character" capable of swapping tales with the best of storytellers was known far and wide. Approaching 40 years of age, with his habits and lifestyle firmly ingrained, it seemed to all who knew him that he would remain a bachelor. But, as usual, he was full of surprises. His forceful personality had often attracted a lady's eye, but few could see through his rough veneer to the cultured and interesting human being that lay beneath. It took an equally strong and interesting personality to do that — one such as that possessed by Williamina Ross Reid.

"Billie," as she was known to her friends, was born on February 7, 1891 at Ashistiel, Scotland on the River Tweed. One of the youngest of thirteen children, she had been brought up on the Ashistiel Estate, the spot where Sir Walter Scott had written the novel *Marmion*. Her father was the factor and chief horticulturalist on the estate, known for his rose and tomato breeding, while her mother was a Highland Scot. As a young lady Billie worked as a nanny and nursemaid, and by the time she was 18 had left for London to perform the same work. Her bright personality won her many friends, among them the noted English actor Harry Lauder.

Never afraid of a challenge, Billie decided to emigrate to Canada late in 1911, probably at the behest of friends who had already done so. She took passage on the ship *Numidian* embarking from Glasgow on January 13, 1912. On arrival, she enrolled in the Red Cross School of

Nursing in Toronto, and graduated in June, 1912 with an award for the highest mark in the General Nursing course. Apparently she worked for some time in Toronto after this, but before long headed west for Saskatchewan, where she found work at a hotel in Rosetown. One of her good friends from the Old Country introduced Billie to a Mrs. Green from Calgary, who invited her new acquaintance to visit on occasion. During these visits the two would sometimes go to Banff, and Mrs. Green often spoke about a wonderful man she knew there named Jimmy Simpson, who she described as being virtually a part of the mountains. Despite Mrs. Green's suggestions that they look him up, Billie said she wasn't interested. As luck would have it, on one visit in March, 1913 they were passing the post office when a rough-and-ready individual who Billie thought "looked like he'd been out in the mountains for years" came out with a big smile and an armful of mail. Billie's first thought was "who would be writing a fellow like that," and she was taken aback when Mrs. Green called out, "Oh, Jimmy — Jimmy Simpson."

Introductions were soon made and Jimmy invited the two ladies over for tea. When they arrived they found some of their host's pals fiercely engrossed in a poker game around the table, but he ignored them, seated the ladies in front of the fireplace, made tea and sat down to chat. Billie's eyes were drawn to the wonders of the room, particularly the big game heads adorning the walls. Noticing her glances, Jimmy pointed at one and said, "That's a moose." She immediately thought her leg was being pulled because that was the way they pronounced "mouse" in Scotland. When she expressed her doubts, they all had a good laugh and the ice was broken. She returned to Jimmy's comfortable home several times over the next few days and a friendship that would develop during the next few years was struck.

Because of the great distance between them, Jimmy and Billie's early relationship would to a great degree be carried on by mail. One of the first letters he sent her after their meeting came by a rather unique method of delivery:

The Ranch, Kootenai Plains
   Had a fine time coming out, got snow blind for three days & could do nothing but sit in the dark, &, I fear, swear. We were both frightfully out

of condition, & consequently did not make the ranch for 5 days. Have been putting in a nice easy time since arrival, building fences & making corrals, with an occasional ride. Am sending this in by Indian so I suppose it will be an interesting study for a fingerprint expert by the time you get it. If the Lord's willing & the devil don't interfere I'll send you a longer one before long; the Indian is waiting for this.

Over the course uf the next year-and-a-half, Billie moved around a good deal, working in various hotels in Regina, Saskatoon and other locations, and on several occasions they lost touch. But always, just as Jimmy was convinced that she had gone back to Scotland or had "thrown him over," another letter would come telling him of her recent movements and activities. That he was smitten was obvious by his letters of reply. In late 1913 he wrote a series that in his clever way hinted directly at his hopes and intentions:

Billy, I miss you awfully, but it cannot be helped I suppose unless you decide to change the miss. . . .

As Banff seems so good to you, Billy, I feel easier about seeing you here again, even if you do go back to Scotland. I am sure that you would not be quite happy there; there would be something lacking. Perhaps the call of the wild, eh? . . .

Don't you think 1914 & Banff & I would be better luck? Hotel life may be all right in moderation, like hanging, but don't you think it's time you had a home of your own?

Billie was not yet totally convinced, and seemed to be worried that there was more than one woman in Jimmy's life. In response, he went to great pains to assure her that such was not the case, pointing out that most of his time in town had been spent with the boys in some of his famous exploits:

No Billy girl, I have not made a hit with the young lady from the hospital; have not seen her for a week. I might be able to get along with her if I had never met you, but that makes all the difference in the world.

But that reminds me that I have a confession to make. I committed a most serious offense for which the police searched high and low for me on the evening of March 4th, no March 5th. According to Kipling some men get "pickled" when the Lord pleases, & I guess I am one of that species. According to reports, maybe exaggerated, maybe not, I was climbing a telephone pole in a fur coat & bowler hat with the crown gone & discoursing earnestly on the epistles of St. John. This was followed by demonstrating my ability to walk a straight chalk line & to referee a hockey game on the sidewalk between boys fifteen to twenty years. I fully believe the latter as my shins were black & blue next day. Isn't it funny how we sometimes fall from grace?

Correspondence of this type continued unabated through 1914. Jimmy invited Billie to visit him at the Kootenay Plains ranch in the spring and then again at the Alpine Club camp he was outfitting in the Yoho Valley in the summer, but she did not come. By the fall he was convinced that he had to take matters into his own hands, writing that "it appears to be a case of Mohamet & the mountain doesn't it?," and telling her he would come to Saskatoon after the completion of the hunting season. That seemed to turn the trick, as even before he returned from the trail in the fall she had moved to Calgary and was soon employed at Pryce Jones, a dry goods store. Their close proximity allowed them to carry on their relationship personally rather than by mail and through 1915 it gradually changed. On returning from the McAleenan trip in early September, he wrote her about the trip and proposed one more time: "I had five of the finest fellows on the last trip & somehow nothing is too good for me. I am to visit them this winter and partake of all they have & they seem to mean it too. I guess I'll have to take you too, eh?" This time she accepted, and at the beginning of October, on departing for the Kootenay Plains, he wrote "as for the beginning of 1916 I shall leave all the details to you."

As to their future home, there was no doubt in either of their minds that it would be Banff and the Rockies. As Jimmy had written in an earlier letter that came as close as he ever did to describing the emotions that the mountains evoked in him, it was what they both wanted:

I know just what your feelings are regarding nature, little girl, because I am the same. Do you think I could go & live in the city after lasting for so long in the beauty of the great outdoors? There is absolutely nothing in the city to give us the same feeling as the great, mysterious things of nature even though they be stone and ice. It is only among them that we feel the utter helplessness and insignificance of ourselves.

Later in life, when asked how it was he and Billie came to be engaged, Jimmy would respond with one of his typical quick-witted rejoinders. He recounted that when he first saw her she was walking down Banff Avenue with her nose in the air and he had to think of some way to attract her attention. He went into Dave White's store, bought a bag of oatmeal, snipped a hole in it and let the oatmeal trickle out all the way home: "Billie followed the trail all down the street — she's Scotch you know — and when she got to my place I nabbed her."

The date for the wedding was set in late January, 1916 and as it approached Jimmy began fixing up his home more to a woman's taste and preparing himself for the changes that his life would undergo. In late December he wrote, "I have been playing too much cards lately, but after February 1st it's quits for keeps." As for his old cronies, they couldn't quite believe it, and he reported that "much speculation is in the air as to whether I am getting married or am a colossal liar. They much favour the latter." McAleenan extended his invitation to host the new Mrs. Simpson as well as Jimmy himself during a trip to New York and wrote a letter that he asked Jimmy to pass along to her. In sending it, Jimmy wrote: "Do not think me the fine person he depicts. I have a thousand faults he does not know of & I think you can break me of them all." Then, on the very eve of the momentous occasion, an event occurred that perhaps more than anything marked the closing of a chapter in his life — Dooley, his old friend and constant companion, died. Jimmy mourned, "I shall bury the old fellow with many regrets, as he was far preferable to most men I have met."

The wedding was held on a very cold and snowy January 31, 1916 at the home of the Reverend S. Bacon Hillocks, a Presbyterian minister, in Calgary. Standing up for the bride and groom were Maude and Joe Woodworth, friends of Jimmy's from the multitudinous family of Banff pioneer Ben Woodworth, and a few other friends were in attendance. Jimmy recorded that "after various dishes of cake & gulps of port wine in which some half dozen assisted we hit the trail for the station," where they caught the early morning train bound for New York. Passage to Montreal and then on to the United States via CPR connections had been arranged by Jimmy in November, 1915 through an approach to John Murray Gibbon, Chief Publicity Agent for the CPR and a frequent visitor to the Rockies. In return for photographs Jimmy had taken and had collected from some of his clients that could be used to advertise the mountains, and on the understanding that he would try to publicly promote the Rockies during his stay in New York, Gibbon was able to provide the transportation for the newlywed couple free of charge.

The five days of travel across the country to Montreal provided a chance for the couple to relax and partake of a "continual round of pleasure — eat, sleep and ride in a Pullman car." On passing through Ottawa, Jimmy read in the paper that the Parliament Buildings had been destroyed by fire, but they "did not see it as we were busily engaged in getting up." A stop-over in Montreal allowed them to attend the theatre and Jimmy hoped to get to a hockey game, but the train schedule would not permit it. On February 6th they arrived in New York and checked into the Belmont Hotel at 42nd Street and Park Avenue as the guests of McAleenan. Here they were to stay for the next two months while they enjoyed the numerous sights and activities of New York. It was to be a continual round of lunches and dinners with the McAleenans, the Rungiuses and other clients who had visited the Rockies, visits to galleries and artists' studios, nights at the theatre, and talks with those who might be convinced to go on a trip — in short, an opportunity to enjoy all the city had to offer and at the same time do a little business.

McAleenan, his wife and family of four boys and two girls took an immediate liking to Billie, and nothing was too good for her. She liked them as well and spent much of her time in their company, often entertaining them with her dramatic talents. The seventh daughter of a seventh daughter, which in Scotland was believed to give a person special powers, she was a remarkable fortune teller with cards and teacups.

Arrangements had been made by McAleenan for Jimmy to show the movies taken the previous fall to the Montauk Club, one of the various organizations he belonged to which he felt would provide his friend with some valuable new connections. The event proved extremely successful and Jimmy recorded in his diary: "Got a credit in the *Brooklyn Daily News* for being a very interesting man. Gross libel." But, as usual, he was being humble about his own abilities, as a reading of the article illustrates:

All this should be about the sportsmen's dinner at the Montauk Club last night and it would be were it not for that soft-spoken, wind-burned mountain man that John Murgatroyd brought over to the press table.

He blew into the club by chance, seeking two or three men with whom he had traveled, and they would not let him go away till the show was over. So while he nibbled a stalk of celery and eyed with interest the multitudinous expanse of starched shirt-fronts around him, Dr. Harlow Brooks and one or two others chatted a bit with him about things up in northwestern Alberta, whence he came. A stranger sauntered over and asked what sort of a place the eastern slope of the Canadian Rockies was to hunt through or live in. Jim Simpson told him.

And as he talked, the smoke that clogged the room with acrid odor faded into the clouds above a mountain top; the cloth on the table was snow, and he made a mountain stream of a silver fork, and with a thumbnail trailed a mountain goat 10,000 feet above sea level on a napkin cone peak. . .

They would not let him escape after the dinner, Murgatroyd, McAleenan, Brooks and the others, but made him stand up and comment for the crowd on a few reels of moving pictures that they took up Alberta way last autumn. So he guided the dinner party of 177 tenderfeet from Lake Louise north 500 miles over pass and glacier, through snowstorm and river ice, and showed them ptarmigan and moose, mountain goat and sheep and brought them back in safety as the switch was swung over again. . .

After that all who knew Jim Simpson thronged about the table at which he sat a guest of honor now, and sought to have the recollection of what they had just heard blown from their minds by a tale or two with clean, cold mountain air sifting through it .

As Jimmy later recalled it, the highlight of the evening for him came when he was showing the audience the movie and the picture on the screen showed a moose walking from sunlight into shadow. Just at that moment one of the members of the audience got up, casting his shadow on the screen, and Jimmy interrupted his narrative with, "Holy Christ, there's another moose crossing into the shadow."

Two nights later, they attended the ladies' evening at the Camp Fire Club held in the Astor Hotel and met many other important people, including Dr. Hornaday. Within his first week of arrival Jimmy had already made a great impression, and in the weeks ahead he built on it by visiting many of these acquaintances in their own homes and offices and attending other dinners. He also spent many afternoons in Carl Rungius' studio talking, getting some pointers on painting and watching him work up the sketch material he had gathered in the mountains into large studio canvases. In so doing he witnessed his own paintings being created, for Rungius owed him one or two from previous summer trips. With the artist and McAleenan he attended several lunches and exhibitions at the Salmagundi (Art) Club, of which Rungius was a member, and on one occasion McAleenan bought a painting entitled *Arizona Desert* by A. L. Groll for $150 and immediately gave it to Jimmy as a present.

But the artistic highlight of the trip came a short time later when they visited the Folsom Galleries to view Charlie Russell's New York exhibition and had the good fortune to meet the artist and his wife Nancy. Jimmy was taken with the works because they were so life-like and every one told a story. He asked Mrs. Russell the price of one that particularly caught his fancy called *The Mankiller* and when she said $75 he immediately bought it. Russell invited them to visit the studio on 42nd Street that he shared with fellow western artist Edward Borein, and a week later they took him up on the offer. The visit would remain fresh in Jimmy's memory for the rest of his life:

He was the most wonderful fellow, full of fun & dry humour. I mentioned to him that he had marvellous hands with long thin fingers just like a musician. "Well," he said, "I used them once as a midwife." I said, "Did you make a success of it?" He replied, "Well, the kid's still living."

His studio was an inch deep in bottle tops and cigarette butts. He was talking to a couple of New Yorkers, telling them a story, when he reached in his pocket and pulled out something and put his hands under the table. He went on talking to them and then put a buffalo made of plasticine on top of a bottle. One of the New Yorkers reached for it, but Charlie got it first, rolled it up and went on talking. A minute later he put up a mountain sheep, beautifully proportioned. He never once looked at what he was doing. That is a born artist.

I asked him if he had ever taken any art lessons. He replied, "Only one — I learned the definition of a straight line." "What is that," I asked. He pointed across the street and said, "See that saloon over there — watch me."

Before he left the studio, Jimmy commissioned another painting. This one was of his saddle horse with the rifle scabbard hanging from the saddle as it would be carried in the Canadian Rockies, different from the way Russell would have painted it in Montana.

The other highlight of the trip for the honeymooners was the opportunity to attend the opera and the theatre. Both of them were avid music fans and Billie had a particular fascination for a good play, something she had not been able to indulge since leaving London. New York provided the best of both worlds and they took full advantage of it. On three different occasions they had the opportunity to hear Caruso sing, and they attended numerous other concerts. They were highly impressed with the violin playing of Mischa Elman, who they found "is the same wonderful player as his records suggest." They also attended several plays and vaudeville acts and Billie proved to be a harsh critic, being impressed by very few. But it was their attendance at a performance of a different sort that would leave the greatest impression on her and create an interest that would play an important role in their future lives. As mentioned, Jimmy had played and coached hockey for several years and was a good skater, but Billie had yet to attempt to master the blades. One evening they attended a skating concert at the Hippodrome featuring "The Great Charlotte," the toast of the figure skating world on the European continent. The performance completely captivated Billie, as the skater seemed to spin right up out of the ice, and she determined on the spot to learn more about this beautiful and dramatic sport.

During their last days in New York, Jimmy and Billie were frequent visitors to the studio and home of Carl Rungius. Despite the outbreak of war in Europe, they felt the Rungiuses were different than the Germans overseas, a point of view strengthened by the fact that Louise Rungius had been born in the United States and Carl had taken out citizenship. The visits were occasioned by the fact that Jimmy had to choose three paintings, one of which he would take home with him, a not inconsiderable decision since some of Rungius' canvases were selling for over $1,000 each by this time. They were also to receive Rungius' wedding present, a bronze mountain sheep. Carl had produced his first bronze, a moose, shortly after the turn of the century and the sheep was to be his second attempt. The first casting was to be the present, but when he showed it to Jimmy the artist noted a look of misapprehension cross Jimmy's face and he asked what was the matter. Jimmy's knowledge of big game anatomy had led him to observe a flaw in the work, and when Rungius asked what it was he said he thought the model had been done from a dead sheep because he could "see the death stretch in the hindquarters." Rungius had tremendous respect for Jimmy's opinion and he decided to correct the mould and rework it before casting the other five bronzes in the edition, which left the Simpsons with a unique wedding gift.

On April 5th, the couple were seen off on the train by McAleenan and Rungius and they headed back to Banff to make their home. Jimmy was well pleased with the results of the trip, having several prospects in hand, and he began laying plans for the season's activities. After arriving home on April 10th he went to work and during the early part of the year Billie accompanied him on some of his trips. But before the summer was over it was apparent that she was pregnant and by the fall hunting season such activities had to be curtailed. That fall proved to be his busiest to date, the main clients being Frothingham, whom he had met in New York, and Dr. Brace Paddock of Pittsfield, Massachusetts. Unfortunately, Paddock and his companion, J. Crawford, arrived rather late in the season and the pack train ran into heavy snows while out on the trail, forcing Jimmy to turn back before his clients had the opportunity to do any hunting.

Because of the obvious success of the previous year's visit to New York, Jimmy laid plans to repeat the trip in early 1917. This time, though, he would go alone, for on January 3, 1917 he and Billie were blessed with the arrival of their first child, Catherine Margaret, known to most as Margaret and to her family as "Peg." As a young baby she was quite a handful for the new mother, but business had to be attended to and Jimmy departed for the east in early March.

Before being in New York two weeks he had almost all the business he could handle and wrote Billie: "If all these people sign up I don't know what I shall do with them. Possibly I can send them playing golf or knitting socks, but I might get you to guide an outfit." The clients included his old pals McAleenan, Brooks and Murgatroyd, who wanted to hunt bear from the Kootenay Plains Ranch in May, 1918, as well as several new people that the continuous round of dinners, lectures and other social events brought him into contact with. One of the most important acquaintances, made through an introduction by Bob Boyd, whom he had met during his previous trip, was with Felix and Otto Kahn of the large banking firm of Kahn and Company, who wished to go on a pleasure trip. This family would play a significant role in his future business and provide him with further entrées into the company of the wealthy and famous.

An equally interesting contact that was re-established during his 1917 trip was with a young woman by the name of Caroline Hinman. During their trip in 1916, Billie and he had attended a dinner held by the New York members of the Alpine Club of Canada at which Jimmy presented a lantern slide lecture. The woman who had arranged this was Mary Jobe, a teacher of history at Hunter College and avid explorer of the northern Rockies, who had penetrated the remote Mount Sir Alexander area with Jasper guide Curly Phillips in 1914. Jimmy had met her at one of the several Alpine Club camps he outfitted. After the dinner, she provided the Simpsons with a driver to take them back to their hotel —

Caroline Hinman, Secretary of the Board of Education in Summit, New Jersey. Hinman had accompanied Jobe on her trip to Mount Sir Alexander and had also attended a couple of Alpine Club camps. After participating in a conducted tour of young girls to Europe, she had decided to form her own conducted tour groups and in 1916 took her first group of girls on the trail in Glacier Park, Montana. Hearing of Jimmy's return to New York, and wishing to extend her trips further afield, she contacted him and asked for ideas about a possible conducted tour in the Canadian Rockies. He gave her some suggestions and she agreed that she would try to interest a group of college age girls in a trip to be outfitted by him for the summer of 1917.

With these contacts in hand, Jimmy grew more optimistic the longer he stayed. He wrote Billie that "In all probabilities I can get near to 4 figures in deposits & may get a $10000.00 season," a heretofore undreamed of level of success. But being away from home and family did not particularly agree with him, something he also alluded to in his letters: "In spite of all I begin to feel as if I would like to see the western landscape again. There is some charm about the Rockies that is indescribable & one feels a longing to see it again. Possibly it is yourself & the kiddie that generates this feeling but it is there just the same." Despite McAleenan, Rungius and the other friends who implored him to extend his visit, he headed for home in mid-April with a new painting from Carl under his arm. On the way he stopped at the CPR offices in Montreal to have some discussions about the government's threat to close off part of his best sheep hunting territory in the Brazeau, a serious affair.

Soon after his return to Banff, Jimmy received a letter from McAleenan expressing concern about an issue that had come up in their discussions in New York. War was raging in Europe, and as the United States would soon enter it there was much talk at the dinners Jimmy attended. McAleenan's concern was with the imposition of conscription in Canada and the fear that it might take Jimmy off to war. After the war had broken out in the fall of 1914 and many young Canadian men had rushed to enlist, Jimmy, at age 37, had decided to wait to see which way the wind blew. In a letter to Billie he wrote that he would not volunteer unless the call was urgent, in which case "I could not resist." He felt that most of the volunteers would only occupy back-up positions while the regulars went to the front, and that did not appeal to him. However, he determined that "an urgent call & a cavalry contingent would catch me at once." By the time matters worsened to the point that he might have considered this course, things had changed. Not only was he beyond the usual age of those called but he also had two dependents, a wife and child. Nevertheless, McAleenan's letter made a generous offer, showing the depth of his feeling: "I do not see how you would be taken for you have two dependant people, but if you are let me know. I promise you upon the altar of friendship where everything that a man holds dear that I will look after your Mrs. and baby Margaret until you get back."

The call for Jimmy never came, although the war soon began to have some effect on his business. The entry of the United States into the conflict meant that several of the parties that he had booked decided to cancel out. One tourist party and two hunting parties informed him during the summer that they would not be coming for this reason. However, his recruiting of clients had been so successful that until these cancellations came in he was not in a position to take out all those who were interested in a trip for 1917, and so he was able to fill in nicely with them. Despite the wartime conditions, the season was even better than the one before.

On September 29, 1917 the local Banff newspaper, *The Crag and Canyon*, ran a front page article on the large number of clients that Jimmy was outfitting and noted the positive effect that his efforts were having on the tourist business in the Banff region. It stated that "two of New York's most noted men, Dr. A. G. Bugbee and Carl Rungius, the noted animal painter, returned on Monday from travelling over the mountains in search of game and subjects for paintings and both are not only satisfied with their trips and the results obtained but are so enthusiastic over the country travelled that they have both determined to make this their annual hunting and holidaying grounds." The article mentioned that Dr. Bugbee and his wife had been out for four weeks with Jimmy as the guide, Jack Powell as the cook and Howard Deegan as the packer in the Cataract River area, while Rungius was outfitted by Simpson for the same area with Jim Boyce as cook and Max Brooks as packer. Both parties bagged some good trophies, and Dr. Bugbee was so enthusiastic that he stated it was "the best and most exciting trip he ever made into the wilds on a hunting trip" and that he had decided "to tell all the people of New York to get out into the country around Banff for splendid game." The story concluded by pointing out that another party outfitted by Simpson, J. T. Crawley of Santiago-de-los-Vegas, Cuba, had just departed for the north on a hunting trip and that if he was successful he would return "as enthusiastic over the country as the two New Yorkers, and this will mean advertising for this country in an entirely different sphere."

With such glowing praise, it is not surprising that Jimmy would begin to plan for a third trip to New York for the early spring of 1918. But those plans had to be changed with the imminent arrival of his second child. Billie had experienced some difficulties with her first pregnancy and so she went into the hospital in Calgary to be close to the best medical care. Their second daughter, christened Mary Louise, was born there on April 9, 1918. The next day Jimmy, who was home caring for the 15-month-old Margaret (whom he had nicknamed "Slippery") and overseeing an enlargement to the house, wrote Billie: "Just got the news of the birth of our new little daughter & I am pleased . . . It will be fine for Slippery to have a sister, because they will have so much in common when they grow up." Little did he realize how prophetic these words would be.

As a consequence of this happy delay, Jimmy did not return to New York until March, 1919. Once again he stayed at the Belmont and made the usual rounds. Soon after arriving he went to lunch with a client, Charlie Smith, and reported to Billie in a letter that it had been "a wet one" and that on retiring to his room he found that it "has been inhabited with blue & pink anacondas and boa constrictors in hobble skirts and high shoes, but they're retiring now & I feel easier." For the most part, he avoided such excesses and spent his time in more cultured activities. He attended the opera with McAleenan, but, generally speaking, spent less time with him than previously.

On this trip, his attention was focussed on the Kahn family, who were planning a major family expedition to the Rockies for the coming summer, and on a new client, Billy Beach, who was interested in taking his first hunting trip under Jimmy's guidance. Otto Kahn was on the

Board of the Metropolitan Opera and Jimmy wrote Billie that "they want me to go down to Long Island for a weekend & the old man wants to supply opera tickets for the Metropolitan whenever I wish." He was to take full advantage of the offer and was able to hear all his favourite singers and musicians, including Caruso, Elmen, Rubinstein, Barrientos, and Heifitz, during his stay.

Beach, the owner of the Pennsylvania Cement Company, the firm that supplied the concrete for the building of the New York subway system, had a reputation as one of the United States' foremost outdoorsmen and big game hunters. He had met Jimmy when, attracted by his reputation as a bighorn sheep guide, he had stopped off to interview him in Banff on a trip to the Cassiar district in British Columbia. Impressed by what he heard, Beach determined to take a trip under Jimmy's guidance, and during his New York stay the two reached an agreement for a hunt and signed a contract on April 11th that laid out the terms, the first time that Jimmy was known to have entered into a legal agreement to provide his services. By its terms the trip was to commence on August 27, 1919 and was to last for five weeks, with Jimmy providing "all conveyance, food, tents, cooking utensils, etc." as well as his personal services as guide, while Beach was responsible for his own hunting license and "personal bedding and requisites." The charges were to be $175 per week, but if Beach were to find another person to join the hunt the rate would be $150 each per week. Beach provided a $100 non-refundable deposit and agreed to give 30 days notice if he was unable to go or a payment of a further $250 in addition to the deposit if notice of cancellation were given less than 30 days before departure. Undoubtedly, these were Jimmy's usual terms for such a trip at the time.

Another positive aspect of the 1919 trip was the cooperation that Jimmy received from the CPR. Not only was transportation provided, as it had been on earlier trips, but this time the company worked hard at making opportunities available for him to promote himself and his business. In one letter he wrote that "I am to meet a representative of the United States Press tomorrow at the Broadway offices of the CPR & will fill him full of western hot air. . . Am meeting lots of people that are new to me & the C. P. R. here are doing all they can for me I know." This was an interesting change in attitude on his part from 1917, when the

New York office of the company had offered him their help and he had refused, telling them "the CPR is too Brewster-ridden for me to be able to do anything ..." Perhaps it was a sign of business and personal maturity brought home to him from his New York visits and leading him to recognize the value of working at getting along with all kinds of people, no matter how difficult it might be, in order to be successful.

When he headed home from New York in mid-April, Jimmy felt that if things continued as they were he would soon have prospects for a $20,000 year in hand. The years of building up his clientele on their own turf were now paying excellent dividends, and his connections were solidly intact. Just how respected he had become among those of consequence in the city was illustrated that fall when Joe McAleenan proposed him for membership in the Campfire Club, referring to him as "a splendid hunter, companion and gentleman," and he was accepted into its exclusive ranks. But despite the assistance of the CPR and the hospitality of his friends the yearly trip to the east was becoming an expensive proposition, and faced with the costs and responsibilities of a growing family he could no longer justify these annual pilgrimmages. Following one last visit to New York in 1920, he would make few major trips outside the Canadian Rockies for the remainder of his life.

*Jimmy and his trailhands skinning a goat near Howse Peak, 1917.
Byron Harmon photograph*

Bow Lake and Glacier, much as it looked when Jimmy first visited and thought, "Some day I'll build a shack here"

Development at Bow Lake required some unique packing methods, as illustrated in this packtrain near the Crowfoot Glacier, ca. 1920

Jimmy's packtrain on the first crossing of the Saskatchewan Glacier,
1923

On the summit of Mt. Columbia, July 14, 1923; l. to r. — Conrad
Kain, J. Monroe Thorington, Jimmy, W. S. Ladd

The skating "Simpson Sisters" practising on Bow Glacier, ca 1937

The octagonal "Ram Pasture," built over the period 1922-24. Bill DeHaan photograph

Jimmy at work on the roof of Num-Ti-Jah, September, 1938

The addition to Num-Ti-Jah under construction, 1949

The Simpson family at Num-Ti-Jah, 1956; Mary, Jimmy jr., Billie, Jimmy

Billie and Jimmy, 1957

Jimmy officially opening the Whyte Museum of the Canadian Rockies, June 15, 1968

*Jimmy Simpson, legend of the Rockies, the last and greatest of the
Canadian mountain men*

CHAPTER SEVEN

New Directions

As the success of Jimmy's promotional efforts and the value of his connections began to pay increasing dividends, with more parties wishing to utilize his services, the nature of these services changed accordingly. In the early years, his small size had allowed him to personally guide each party booked, using one or two of the numerous able-bodied trailmen in Banff as assistants. But as the number and size of the groups he outfitted began to grow, he wasn't always able to accompany them personally and needed more men to help him. The personal services aspect was a difficult one, particularly with hunters who had heard of his prowess as a big game guide and insisted that he accompany them before they agreed to outfit with him. This required some juggling — Jimmy often spent part of a trip with one party and then moved on to spend part with another. However, what he needed most was to find capable and trustworthy men to guide, pack and cook for parties that he was not able to accompany. During the decade, several interesting individuals who would go on to establish enviable reputations as trailmen and outdoorsmen got their start working for Jimmy in this way.

In his early years as an outfitter, Jimmy mostly used fellow Englishmen like Syd Baker, Sid Unwin and Ernie Brearley as assistants on his trips. Baker and Unwin both went into business for themselves before 1910 and his most reliable man after that was Brearley. Unfortunately, they had a difference of opinion, and in 1914 Jimmy wrote: "Ernie is not with me this year as he is starting out himself & is I think in the Laggan district. We differed last summer & as he knew how to run my business better than I did myself I gave him a chance to run his own. But I sure hope he makes good." Such partings were inevitable among men of such strong character and independent spirit as those who followed the trail; once they had learned the necessary skills most wished to branch out on their own. Many of those who worked for Jimmy over the years did so, as he had done so himself in leaving Wilson, but in most cases it did not mean the end of their friendship.

Replacing these English immigrants and providing the new corps of manpower for his growing business were mainly younger, Canadian-born men. Initially most of them were drawn from the rather large ranks of the pioneer Banff family of Benjamin Woodworth. Ben Woodworth, a native of Nova Scotia, had first come to Banff during railroad construction days in 1883, and after its completion had worked as a stable boss, first for the CPR and then later for Dr. R. G. Brett at the Sanitarium Hotel. He had also gone out on the trail for Tom Wilson on a couple of occasions and in 1910 received the appointment as caretaker at the government buffalo paddock at the foot of Cascade Mountain. Woodworth's marriage in Banff in 1888 resulted in a large family, five girls and six boys, and as he was a friend of Jimmy's it was not surprising that as the boys became young men they should find employment on his crew. The eldest, Ben, began to work for him about 1912, as did the second oldest, Joe, and a few years later they were joined by a third brother, Percy, or "Beef" as he was known because of his penchant for trail grub.

While not Woodworths themselves, two of Jimmy's most important employees during these years came to him through their relationship with this family as well. Ulysses LaCasse had been born in Winchester, Ontario in 1888 and had grown up in Seaforth before moving west to Medicine Hat when he was 18. He first arrived in Banff in 1908 and worked as a cook at a lumber camp before putting in a year at Camrose as a baker's apprentice. When he returned to Banff he worked as a baker for Brewsters and began courting one of the Woodworth daughters, Annie, whom he would marry in 1918. His first trip on the trail came in 1911 when he accompanied outfitter Frank Wellman as cook for a Doctor Kyle and his patient Jack Poclain, son of the owner of the Baldwin Locomotive Works. In 1913 he worked for A. O. Wheeler as a cook on the B.C. - Alberta Boundary Survey and the next year he joined Jimmy as a packer and cook to assist with the outfitting of the

Alpine Club camp in the Yoho Valley. "The Frog," as he was known to all, proved himself immediately, and within a year Jimmy was confident enough of his abilities to promote him to guide. For the next few years, when there was a party that Jimmy could not guide himself, it was usually put under LaCasse's direction. His pleasing personality endeared him to many customers, and the members of the McAleenan party in particular enjoyed him. As a result, during Jimmy's 1917 visit to New York, LaCasse joined him for a time to assist with the public relations chores.

One of the most important parties LaCasse guided for Simpson came about as a result of the contact Jimmy made with Caroline Hinman on this New York trip. Jimmy had so much potential business lined up by the time Miss Hinman approached him that he confided in Billie that he didn't know if he would have enough men to handle it, but that he would use another outfitter on a commission basis if necessary. By the time she arrived in Banff in early August, though, the manpower situation had been worked out satisfactorily and he assigned LaCasse as head guide, assisted by Jim Boyce, Max Brooks and Howard Deegan, to escort Miss Hinman and her party of nine young ladies on what amounted to a three-week circle trip. Jimmy accompanied them the first day from Banff to Whiteman's Pass and then turned over responsibility to LaCasse, and he performed admirably throughout the rest of the trip.

The strategy of the party was to move continuously for a few days until an interesting place was reached and then to spend a couple of days relaxing at it. The group spent four days at Mount Assiniboine before heading north by Simpson Pass, Healy Creek, Mt.Edith and Sawback Lake to the Panther River, where another stopover was made, and then by way of the Red Deer River to the Ptarmigan Valley, where the final layover was made before finishing up at the Chateau Lake Louise. Many evenings at camp the men, little older than the girls they were accompanying, showed off and "did lots of wrestling stunts and nearly killed themselves" as one of the girls, Mavis Benedict, noted in her diary. She marvelled at the way LaCasse could teach his horse tricks, commenting that "he is just like a circus pony." Some of the guides' antics became quite involved, particularly when they related to the girls' constant fear of bears:

Hazle, Betty, and I were sitting and singing around the fire and the others were watching Boyce make bannock. All of a sudden I heard a noise in the bushes then they all did and we called for LaCasse. He came casually but brought his pistol along and then they all came up. They listened a minute then Jim said, "It's a bear," and they tore off in the direction of the noise. Soon we heard three shots and more scrambling, then they appeared carrying the "bear." Our only bear turned out to be Deegan dressed up with chaps on his legs and arms and a black scarf on his head. My knees continued to shake for some minutes later.

While they were very lighthearted and entertaining in camp, during the day the men were all business and extracted the girls, who were new to riding and the ways of the trail, from some ticklish situations. Over the course of the trip they learned to enjoy trail life and as they neared its end Mavis Benedict noted that it was sad to leave but that "it helped a lot to think that we would be East for awhile but next summer would see us in the Rockies." And indeed she was right, for Miss Hinman was so pleased with the results of Jimmy's services and the capabilities of the men he supplied that she would call on them again for the next two years. In fact, this trip was the first of several decades of "Off The Beaten Track" tours that she would accompany in the Rockies; these tours were to become one of the mainstays of Jim Boyce's business when he went out on his own in the early twenties.

Another valuable find first introduced to Jimmy by the Woodworth family was Tommy Frayne. Born in 1887 in Northwich, Cheshire, England, he first came to Canada in 1907 and to Banff in 1911, where he too initially worked for Dr. Brett driving a team. For three years he drove for the Brewster company, carriages in the summer and 30-horse teams working on the Bow River ice harvest in the winter. About 1914 he was asked, along with Beef Woodworth, to assist John Wilson with one of his pack parties and the next year they were both asked by Simpson to join him. Tommy's first job was to assist with the horse breaking on the Kootenay Plains, after which he was put on as "grub boy" at $60 per month on some of Jimmy's trail parties. Like his confrére LaCasse, his personality was such that he meshed perfectly with Jimmy's team of men, as well as with the dudes that he accompanied. Soon he had earned the nicknames "The Sparrow," and "The English Nuisance," and he would work as a cook for Jimmy perhaps longer than any other man he ever employed.

Several other young men from Banff joined Jimmy in the same period, and worked for him for varying lengths of time. Among them were George "Mousie" Saddington, Ernie Stenton, Jim Boyce, Howard Deegan and Max Brooks. But it was one of the three original Woodworth boys, 20-year-old Joe, who would form the closest friendship with his boss, leading to the request that he stand up at Jimmy's and Billie's wedding. Joe's experiences provide examples of both the normal and the unusual in one working for Simpson at this time. They began in the fall of 1912, after his regular job at Dr. Brett's stables was over for the season, and initially involved helping out with the work at the Kootenay Plains ranch:

In the fall of 1912, after the Bretton Hall stable closed for the winter, James Simpson and John Wilson were preparing to take their pack and saddle horses from Lake Louise to the Kootenay Plains, some 65 miles north of Lake Louise, for winter pasturage. Mr. Simpson asked me to go on this trip. This was my start of three years of mountain trips with pack horses...

At the time of my first trip to the Plains there were approximately two hundred head of horses, in four bands, running free on the area. These had to be rounded up, colts branded; fences checked and repaired where necessary. Following completion of all chores we would return to Lake Louise on foot.

On the final trip to the Kootenay Plains each fall it was necessary to pack in sufficient food supplies to meet the requirements of the crew that would return to the Plains the following spring, usually six men. This crew would round up the horses, break to saddle or pack those that were three years old, and carry out any other chores necessary on the ranch. The horses to be used in the outfitting business that summer by both Mr. Simpson and John Wilson would be rounded up and put in a fenced pasture ready for the return to Lake Louise.

Joe was one of the six who returned in the spring of 1913 and he spent that summer learning how to pack on some of Jimmy's trips. He caught on quickly and the next summer, along with Jim Boyce, a lad from Pembroke, Ontario who had come to Banff in 1911 to join his father, a trail-building contractor, he was assigned to assist with one of Jimmy's most ambitious parties to date. This was composed of two ladies, Mrs. Crandell and Mrs. Chandler of Philadelphia. Mrs. Crandell was supposed to have accompanied Mary Schäffer and her party on the trip in 1908 when Maligne Lake was discovered, but she had been forced to withdraw when she took ill at the last moment. She had arranged with Jimmy to provide an outfit, so that she could retrace the route using the map that Mrs. Schäffer had published in her book *Old Indian Trails of the Canadian Rockies*.

The party, composed of five saddle and ten pack horses with sufficient provisions to last for six weeks, left Lake Louise on July 10, 1914 under the guidance of Jack Greaves. Jimmy had never travelled as far north as Maligne Lake, but he had gathered information from the guides on the Schäffer trip, Billy Warren and Sid Unwin. Joe Woodworth recalled that some of the trails travelled were well known and well marked, particularly as far as the Brazeau, but after that the way became fainter and they had to rely frequently on the map in Mrs. Schäffer's book. Eventually he and Boyce discovered the stream that was the key to finding the lake, and the quest was successful. The return to Lake Louise involved a different route that included a visit to Pinto Lake and a trip down the Cline River to the Kootenay Plains, where they planned to rest at the ranch before completing the final leg of the journey. Here Woodworth witnessed one of the most puzzling things he ever saw during his days on the trail:

Shortly after camp was made in the pasture of the Simpson-Wilson ranch, we were visited by a number of Indians from the Silas Abraham band who had followed us across the river. We immediately began laying out the material that had become wet in the river crossing so that it would dry in the sun. Throughout the trip Mrs. Crandell was carrying a rather large leather bag, hung by a strap from the pommel of her saddle. This bag she opened and spread the contents out to dry. The Indians, as well as the crew, were greatly surprised at the sight of the contents she spread on the grass, well over one thousand dollars in American bills.

The experience Woodworth gained on this trip made him even more valuable to Jimmy, and he convinced him to stay on the crew the next year. Jimmy liked and admired the boy and the two hit it off well. On one trip down the Spray Valley in 1915 they got into some mischief because of their shared fondness for good trail food and both had to pay the price. The event occurred in camp one day when cook Ernie Hoggard decided to make a jello, one of the staples of the trail cook's repertoire. Jimmy described the result:

While we were camped at Spray Lakes, Ernie Hoggard, the cook, made a jello and put it in the creek to harden. I said to Joe Woodworth, "what about we go down and mop up that jello," and we did. At suppertime Hoggard went down to the creek and came back with a jello. He said that he had made one and had gone down to the creek to see if it was setting and had found a frog in it so he made another one. We ate it up and never told him what we had done, but it tasted good just the same.

Joe stayed in Jimmy's employ until the fall work was completed at the Kootenay Plains in October, 1915, after which he went to Calgary and joined the 82nd Battalion, Canadian Expeditionary Forces. He was in training there at the time he was Jimmy's best man, and remained there until he was shipped overseas in May, 1916. In August, 1916 he was assigned to the 102nd Battalion as a reinforcement, and when the scout officer learned of his mountain occupation he asked him to join the scout section. These men were chosen because of their good sense of direction, ability at observation and organization, and willingness to obey orders, all skills Joe had learned well working for Jimmy. His job was normally carried out at night and involved gathering intelligence in the "no man's land" between his own and the enemy's front line trenches. He successfully carried out this activity during the fighting on the Somme, but during action at the Battle of Vimy Ridge on April 9, 1917 he was hit and had his right arm shattered to the elbow. He lay wounded in a shell hole all day expecting his three fellow scouts to come back for him, but they were all killed during the battle. That night he crawled back to Canadian lines and was evacuated to a hospital, where his right arm was amputated at the elbow. Gangrene set in and several operations were necessary, resulting in two further amputations, that left only a four inch stump. Joe went through a long period of recuperation before he was awarded the Military Medal and discharged from service in March, 1918. Jimmy's old employee Sid Unwin was not so lucky — he was hit by shrapnel at Vimy Ridge the same day as Joe was wounded and died in hospital shortly afterwards.

Some efforts had been made during Joe's recuperation to help him overcome his disability, but most of what he learned was self-taught. Although he was promised a government job, it did not come through until 1922 and in the meantime he had to earn a living. He tried several things, including selling life insurance for a short time, but soon Jimmy asked him to consider returning to work on the trail and convinced him that in spite of the problems of packing with one arm, he would be as valuable as ever. After a warm-up trip with the third Caroline Hinman party Jimmy outfitted, Joe joined him on a Billy Beach hunting trip. In a magazine article that Beach wrote later, he marvelled at Joe's perseverance and adaptation:

Glancing from Jim, my eyes lighted on Joe Woodworth, my friend's guide-to-be. Joe was formerly a scout in the Canadian Army, and bears the mark of the Hun, having lost his right arm at the shoulder. He's the typical man of the mountains, over six feet and clean of limb, though his face shows signs of what he has been through; eight months in "No Man's Land" is bound to leave its trace.

It did not take many days for us to discover that the lost arm had no effect on his efficiency, as there was nothing he wouldn't tackle, and, what is more, was always successful in accomplishing what he undertook. Packing a horse alone had no terrors for him, nor, by the same token, sewing a patch on his trousers; he certainly measured up right.

During this trip, Joe also showed the faith in him had not been misplaced, for while Jimmy was out guiding Beach up one valley near the head of the Brazeau, Joe was guiding his friend, Bill Morden, up another valley, and found him a good ram to take. Beach's admiration took on a more tangible form the next spring when Joe accompanied Jimmy on his last trip to New York and the financier presented Joe with a beautiful Colt revolver in recognition of his sacrifice.

Joe's last year with Jimmy included a rather unique and memorable hunting trip. During his visits to New York, Jimmy had made an arrangement to take Dr. Frank Knause on a spring grizzly bear hunt. Because of a heavy snowfall on the eastern slopes during the winter of 1919-20, it was apparent that his usual spring bear hunting district, the Kootenay-Simpson River area, was not going to be accessible. Jimmy therefore turned to fellow outfitter and guide George Harrison, a former Brewster employee who now operated out of Glacier, B.C., for assistance. Jimmy knew from experience, including his own work on the CPR in the Rogers Pass, that the area around Stoney Creek was excellent for grizzlies, but he was unable to take a client there himself because he did not have a B.C. guide's license. For many years he argued strongly with the B.C. game authorities that he should be able to take parties out on either side of the B.C.-Alberta border, but the provincial regulations stated that the outfitter had to run his business out of B.C. to qualify. Sub-contracting Harrison, who possessed such a license, was a clever but somewhat expensive way around this restriction.

Joe accompanied Harrison to Glacier ten days in advance of Simpson and Knause's arrival in order to set up the hunting camp. When they disembarked from the train at the siding they had to put on their snowshoes, and when they reached Harrison's house to gather the equipment the snow was so deep that they simply opened a second-storey window and went right in. The same heavy snow made access up Stoney Creek extremely difficult, and it took the pair an entire week to tramp down a good trail to the point where the valley opened up a bit. However, after Jimmy and the hunter arrived, new trail had to be broken each day to gain access to the valley where the hunt would take place, and the entire party returned to the camp at the siding each night. After three days of this the trail penetrated far enough into the valley to allow some hunting to begin, and Jimmy, Harrison and the doctor spent two exhausting days on snowshoes before sighting a grizzly. Knause hit him, but not in a vital spot, and the remainder of that day plus the two following were spent tracking the wounded animal through the snow. He was never found, nor were any other grizzlies spotted, probably because they had abandoned the valley on hearing Knause's shots. Such were the vagaries of the life of a hunting guide.

Later that year, Joe and several other of Simpson's men were given another unusual task, clearing trees and bush around his favourite camping area at Bow Lake, where the stream draining Bow Pass entered it. This was occasioned by a variety of circumstances that had occurred in Jimmy's life, including the fate of the Kootenay Plains ranch, changes to his favourite sheep hunting haunt, and his relationship with the first Commissioner of Dominion Parks, J. B. Harkin.

Jimmy had high hopes when he became involved in the Kootenay Plains ranch in 1911, but the reality never quite matched up to expectations. The problem was not with the horses, as they found the surroundings to their liking and prospered accordingly. Rather, the difficulties lay in the relationship between Jimmy and the Wilson family, and their inability to obtain a lease from the Alberta government on the ranch lands. Although John Wilson and he had gone into partnership on the ranch, the arrangement did not extend to their respective outfitting businesses, each of which operated independently. While they would periodically help each other out, they were really in competition much of the time, and there was a fair amount of jealousy and distrust on both sides. This was aggravated by the fact that as time went by the Wilsons' portion of the ranch came back under the control of Tom Wilson, with whom Jimmy had a more difficult time seeing eye to eye.

As the original "squatter" on the Plains, Tom Wilson had the best chance of convincing the government that a lease should be granted, but the province, anxious to control lands in the forestry districts, continually refused to give one. However, they did admit that Wilson had some rights and offered to compensate him by granting some lands in a more settled agricultural area. As time went on, it became apparent to Jimmy that the situation was becoming untenable, and he began to search for a way out. In February, 1918 he entered into discussions with Frank Wellman, an acquaintance from Banff who had operated a dairy and had done a bit of outfitting himself before moving to Morley to take up ranching prior to the war. The result was that Wellman paid him $150 as an option to purchase for $3000 his half interest in the horses, improvements and rights on the ranch, with the option to expire on June 15, 1918.

In the intervening period, the Wilsons also negotiated with Wellman and ultimately, on June 12, 1918, an agreement was reached between the three parties that would see Wellman buy "a mixed bunch of horses consisting of one hundred and forty head now running on the ranch known as the Kootenay Plains Ranch and having the powderhorn brand" for $5,000. Simpson and Wilson were to receive $1,500 cash each immediately, Simpson was to pay Wilson $300 cash, apparently as a settlement of the balance remaining on the original purchase, and the balance was to be paid by Wellman on the delivery of the horses in the fall. Jimmy received $1,650 from Wellman on June 15th, $150 for his option and $1,500 for his initial payment, but soon afterwards the entire deal became mired in litigation. Although the ultimate results are not known, it is certain that Wilson and Simpson sued Wellman, probably for the balance of the $5,000, and Wilson sued Simpson, probably for the balance owing from the original purchase of his half interest. In May, 1919 Wilson signed a surrender of claim to the ranch lands in return for a half section of land in the Peace River district. There is no record of Jimmy ever being compensated for whatever rights he had to the land.

The final result of the fiasco was that Jimmy lost some money, he no longer had a headquarters for his wilderness operations, and he had to incur additional expenses. These included the registration of his own horse brand (IK on the right thigh), and the annual costs of leasing government grazing lands or paying a rancher, at $5 a head, to care for his stock in the winter. About this time, he acquired a section of land in an area between Kootenay and Yoho Parks, but this could in no way be considered an adequate replacement for the ranch. That would come as a result of his relationship with J. B. Harkin, Commissioner of Dominion Parks.

Harkin, a farsighted civil servant who almost singlehandedly created the first Dominion Parks Branch and who was a tireless worker for conservation, became Commissioner in 1912. Harkin was a former newspaperman and a gregarious individual, and when he met Jimmy during a visit to Banff the two hit it off immediately. They shared a number of interests and some acquaintances, including Dr. Hornaday, C. Hart Merriam of the U. S. Biological Survey and other leaders of the conservation movement in the United States. Jimmy respected Harkin, but was not a big supporter of his policy of increasing the size of parks, as he felt that the department already had more land than it could properly manage. Of course, this opinion was undoubtedly partly due to the fact that some of the land in Rocky Mountains Park was formerly part of his favourite hunting and trapping grounds. Harkin likewise seemed to have a grudging admiration for Jimmy, although he sometimes chided him for his activities and opinions. When Harkin expressed his concern about Jimmy's poaching conviction in 1916 and the hope that the $126 fine would deter him, Jimmy's response was, "Oh, don't worry about the money, I took enough game out of your park to make up for it the next month."

One of the most immediate pressures on Harkin when he became Commissioner was to reverse the boundary reductions that had taken place in several parks in 1911. Game protection organizations and officials of the two railways running through Jasper Park were the most vociferous, even though the reductions had taken place in the name of more efficent game protection. After he had thoroughly acquainted himself with the question, Harkin came down in favour of expansion and in 1914 was successful in having the boundaries of Jasper and Waterton Parks extended. A new area added to Jasper Park was around the headwaters of the Brazeau, the new boundary being described as running northeasterly from the height of land in the Columbia Icefield "thence northeasterly following the said height of land to the head waters of Brazeau river; thence northeasterly following the right bank of the Brazeau river to its junction with Southesk river. . ." This effectively cut out a significant portion of Jimmy's favourite sheep hunting range.

Jimmy took every opportunity to let Harkin know how adversely this decision affected him, and also spent a considerable amount of effort lobbying Alberta game commissioner Benjamin Lawton on the subject. But his arguments had little effect, even though he came up with one, based on his knowledge of bighorn sheep habits and the territory in question, that caught both men's attention. His position was that at the same time as the boundary change spoiled much of the bighorn ram hunting, it put the female breeding stock at risk from poachers and Indians. This was because during the major portion of the year when they were not breeding the rams frequented the area included in the park while the ewes and lambs were further south in the Cataract River area outside the park.

It was in 1919, when Jimmy was pressing this argument most persistently, that he approached Harkin with a request of a different nature. Pointing out that the government had effectively constrained his livelihood by eliminating former hunting and trapping areas twice within 12 years, he asked that he be granted a lease on his favourite camping spot at Bow Lake. Jimmy knew he would have a sympathetic ear because Harkin was a strong advocate for the development of tourism in Canada's national parks, stating that recreational opportunities would benefit the health of Canadians and would make the parks valuable economically for the country. Accordingly, in June, 1919 he had approved the application of Frank Wellman and William Potts for a lease of land on Upper Kananaskis Lake for the erection of "cabins for camping purposes."

Jimmy made his official request through the Park Superintendent on July 25, 1919, asking for "3 acres of ground at the Upper Bow Lake for the purpose of erecting suitable buildings for the development of the tourist business." Harkin indicated that he would be willing to release two acres on a yearly permit until such time as $5,000 of work was done, at which point a lease could be considered. Jimmy regarded two acres as inadequate and in November, 1919 wrote Harkin telling him so in no uncertain terms: "This amount is totally inadequate & could only result in an inferior structure that would be of no beauty to the Park & useless as a business venture. It would be impossible to put a building costing some $5,000 on two acres together with outbuildings, stables & corrals unless the whole thing looked more like a Galician homestead than a tourist attraction." In the same breath, he took the opportunity to ask that the size of the parcel be increased to ten acres.

Duly impressed, Harkin set the bureaucratic wheels in motion to examine Jimmy's request and seemed favourably disposed to making more land available. However, this required some sort of a survey and staking of the proposed area, as well as a plan for its development. This took time and it was not until April, 1920 that Jimmy submitted a plan for a rectangular log building, containing a large high-ceilinged studio with fireplace, two bedrooms and a kitchen, and it was August before the ground was satisfactorily staked out for what he thought was the compromise he had arrived at with parks officials, a five acre plot. A lease agreement was sent to him in September, and when he read it he noted, much to his chagrin, that he had miscalculated and had shown only two-and-a-half acres on his plan. A quick letter to the Superintendent asking for reconsideration followed, and it was therefore not until September, 1921 that he entered into a lease agreement for what finally turned out to be a parcel slightly over four acres in area. By its terms he was granted a one year lease on the proviso that within one year he would erect the $5,000 worth of improvements. He would then be granted a twenty-one year lease retroactive to September, 1921.

As was to become his habit at Bow Lake, Jimmy had not waited for all the details to be settled before he set to work. There was a very practical reason for this — he knew that if he waited for the authorities to complete all the paperwork he would lose most, if not all, of each short building season. The task began with him assigning some of his men to clear the timber and willow on the site for the cabin in 1920. Joe Woodworth recalled that the crew, consisting of Simpson, himself, his brothers Ben and Beef, and Howard Deegan, camped at the lake while the work was being carried out. When it was well advanced, the others went to Banff to get a boat from Bill Mather, who ran the Bow River Boathouse, while he stayed put to watch the horses and do a little more clearing. The four returned a few days later almost totally exhausted from having to line, pole and row the boat upstream all the way from Lake Louise to Bow Lake. Eventually the boat was to be used for transporting dudes, but at this point it was needed to avoid having to pack building materials around the muskegy shores of the lake.

When Jimmy and his men were not engaged with a pack trip, they worked at getting out the logs for the cabin. Permission was received to use dead timber from the surrounding area for logs, which was convenient, but because of the altitude at Bow Lake the timber tended to be thick at the butt and then to taper off rapidly to a thin end, not the ideal situation for building logs. To overcome the constraint that this would put on the size of the building, Jimmy came up with a unique design — an octagonal shape. This allowed the logs to be cut to a size where they could carry the weight, about ten feet, and where the diameter remained constant enough to allow a fairly good fit after chinking. The design had an added advantage related to the strong winter winds that often swept down off the Bow Glacier; the straight four-sided structure originally planned would have presented a larger flat surface for snow to drift against, while with the octagonal design the wind could sweep around the building and the drifting problem would be minimized.

Because of these changes, difficulties in transporting materials and the press of business, actual construction on the main cabin was delayed. As a temporary measure, in 1922 Jimmy constructed a 12-foot square gazebo-like frame building covered in mosquito netting from wood he had scrounged from the hoardings around the new construction at Chateau Lake Louise. Ingeniously, he sawed the planks into six foot lengths and then augured holes in them so that they could be loaded onto a pack saddle and firmly attached by a ring bolt for the rough slog up the Bow to the lake. In the fall of 1922, he wrote to the Superintendent and asked for a one-year extension for building the main cabin, noting that he had "placed twelve concrete footings for a 24 ft. building with a four foot open fireplace and a 30 ft. verandah" and that he had "cement, tools, some lumber and other necessaries on the ground ready for work next June and intend to pack in with toboggan in April flooring and doors." Approval was granted for the extension.

Having built a number of trapping cabins over the years, Jimmy had some experience in log work, but the summer of 1923 was heavily booked and he could not afford much time to be personally involved in the construction. Fortunately, in 1920 he had hired an interesting Danish immigrant named Vern Castella to work for him as cook. Castella had apprenticed as a ship's carpenter as a young man and had spent much of his early life at sea in this occupation. When he arrived in Calgary in 1911, he worked on the construction of several major buildings in the city, including the Empress Hotel and the Ross Block, before spending a number of years working on ranches in the Crossfield area. Several of Jimmy's men, but mainly Mousie Saddington, worked with Castella on the log part of the building, but it was when it came time to do roof and the finishing that his carpentry skills became particularly valuable.

In the meantime, when he was not out with a party, Jimmy spent his time packing lumber and building materials from the Lake Louise station to Bow Lake. All the lumber would arrive at the station in long pieces and the station master would contact him to advise on how many pack horses were going to be needed to haul it. Jimmy would arrive at the station with the required number and his saw so that he could cut it down into the six foot lengths that could be carried on a pack saddle. Loading it on his horses was tricky, but that was the least of his trials, as packing almost anything up the notorious 24 mile piece of the Bow Valley trail north of Lake Louise, much less something as unwieldy as these materials, was a battle.

The problem of paying for $5,000 of improvements, as the lease demanded, had been at least partially solved in 1921. Henry Simpson, the uncle who had raised him, died in England that year and left him one-sixth of a fairly substantial estate. Work proceeded rapidly over the summer of 1923 and in October Jimmy reported that the 24 foot by 24 foot octagonal cabin with shingle roof, four windows and a door had been completed and that he expected to have work finished on the fireplace and verandah by the following July. As well, he reported that he had also completed a 14 foot by 16 foot log boathouse. This was not good enough for the government and they refused to grant a full lease, although they did agree to a further one-year extension. In August, 1924 he reported that work had been completed on the main cabin, or "Ram Pasture" as it became known, that he had the materials on hand to begin work on a second 14 foot by 18 foot structure, and that he was having plans prepared for "a ten (10) roomed structure on the main part of the ground."

An inspection by Assistant Superintendent James Woods in October, 1924 resulted in an estimate of $4,000 as the amount of work accomplished and once more the parks branch refused to issue the lease until the full $5,000 was in place. Jimmy's reaction was undoubtedly unprintable, but he had no choice but to comply, and it was not until July, 1925 that Supervising Warden Jack Warren once again inspected the property and advised that with the completion of the second log cabin with fireplace and verandah the required amount of improvements were in place. Accordingly, on September 1, 1925 a 21-year "odd parcel lease" was issued on the Bow Lake lands (NE 1/4 of Sec. 22, Twp. 31, W of 5th) under the authority of the Forest Resources and Park Act, 1911 at an annual rental of $40. A few years later, in 1927, he was issued an additional ten year permit to build a small ancillary camp at Hector Lake for the convenience of summer fishing parties.

With all the vicissitudes of getting the lease at Bow Lake, Jimmy may not have realized that obtaining these rights would be the cornerstone to his family's future. Coincidental with his involvement in this matter, the first automobiles were gaining entry into Rocky Mountains Park, and with Harkin's vision of the role of tourism in the parks changes were afoot that would begin to affect Jimmy's ability to survive solely as an outfitter and guide. Jimmy always said he was lucky, and Bow Lake may have been one of the luckiest things ever to happen to him. But it was accompanied by another bit of good fortune that would make Bow Lake's potential realizable. On November 11, 1921 Billie and Jimmy were blessed with the birth of their third child, a boy named James Gordon, or "Young Jimmy" after his father. With Jimmy approaching the half-century mark in age, it would be through his son and his daughters, Margaret and Mary, that the Simpsons would be able to carry on their business and reach some of the goals that might otherwise have been unattainable.

CHAPTER EIGHT

Mountain Sheep and Mountain Peaks

Coincidental with laying the foundations for his future livelihood by beginning development at Bow Lake, Jimmy was reaping rewards from his unsurpassed reputation as an outfitter and guide. By 1920 his name was synonymous with bighorn sheep hunting in the southern Canadian Rockies, a fame spread far and wide in the numerous outdoors magazine articles written by his eastern American clientele. Notoriety led to a cadre of new hunting clients, and they were joined by a new group of pleasure trip customers anxious to take an outing under Jimmy's guidance. Mountaineering enthusiasts, a type of party that had been absent from his business for a number of years, also began to reappear in his annual pack train registers. Together, these three client groups would combine to mark the twenties as the height of Jimmy's trail career. The magazine articles not only recounted Jimmy's success at leading hunters to their trophies, but also described his great knowledge of sheep habits and habitat, his ability to lead a flawless stalk in difficult conditions and his uncanny ability to sense the presence of game before it was seen. This last attribute was perhaps best described by Billy Beach during one of his hunts in the Brazeau:

We had moved camp and were all seated about the fire telling Rosey how to cook the evening meal. Jim rose and remarked that he felt there were rams in the neighborhood, picked up his glasses and looked up on the mountain-side. We were paying no attention to Jim, but all came up with a jump when he remarked, "I see eight good rams just above camp." All glasses came out and there was great activity, ending in Jim and my companion starting after the rams.

In later years, Jimmy was often asked about this ability and he would recount several instances where it had occurred. On one occasion he was napping in the afternoon sun with his back against a rock, facing away from a mountain range to the west, when he dreamed of two black bears crossing a snow slide. When he awoke he looked around and there were the two bears about a mile away. Another time he was on top of a mountain shoulder glassing for sheep and, seeing nothing, he sat down to rest. A short while later he got the feeling that something was passing above him, and getting up he turned to see a mountain goat crossing within 100 yards of him. Jimmy claimed that a medical friend told him that such powers made him a throwback to prehistoric man, who had an "instinct with nature" because of his dependence on it. Jimmy was pleased to be thought of in that regard, and often quoted the story to the curious.

Clients' stories about Jimmy's almost superhuman hunting abilities were only amplified when word of his most successful hunt ever found its way to the ears of the sporting fraternity. This occurred in 1920, when he secured the world's record bighorn sheep. By Jimmy's account, it was once more a case of his old friend Lady Luck being on his side:

I was out one evening and it was getting very dusk. It was the 2nd of November — the season had ended the 31st of October but I was still out. I saw a very large mountain sheep running toward me in the middle of a rock cliff and I wondered why he was running so much, especially toward me. He must have been scared by something behind him. I hadn't seen anything yet but I knew by the sky I wouldn't have time to stalk that big ram, I'd have to see where he was another day.

I went back to camp and the next morning went out before breakfast to see if I could see him. From where he had been running I hadn't seen 15 more large rams feeding and lying down. He had joined the 15, making the 16th. It was just before the rut comes on, usually in the first week of November, according to climatic conditions. When I saw him, he was riding on top of another large ram. I knew my gun perfectly and I sneaked up to within 50 yards as he hopped on this ram again. I pulled down on him and I was actually pulling the trigger when he dropped down on the ground again. I tried to snap the trigger down and evidently shot over the top.

They all went off on the dead run. I tried to pick him out but I hit between his legs, over top or to one side. Finally they went out of sight. I thought to myself "you damn fool, here you see the biggest thing you've ever seen in your life, you have him dead to rights and you go and miss him." I went up the hillside to see if there was any blood in the light snow. I went up quite a way and was going to turn back when I noticed that one track had turned off from the main bunch. I went along a little way and saw a little blood and thought I had just creased something. I went to the top of a hill to see if I could see anything and here's the world's record ram standing underneath a rock cliff, watching me come with a split foot that he had caught in the fusillade.

The ram was quickly gathered in and as soon as he saw its head Jimmy knew that it was something special. It had a 49 1/2 inch curl and his suspicion that it was a record was confirmed when he got it into town. But despite the fame that he knew would soon come his way from having taken such a trophy, Jimmy's attitude was that it was merely an asset of particularly high value for one in his trade. Therefore, the first step was to have the head properly mounted, and for that he wanted the best taxidermist in North America, James L. Clark of New York. Clark had heard through the outdoorsman's grapevine that Jimmy had taken the sheep and had approached him about mounting it and possibly selling it for him. The first step was to have it delivered, and that was accomplished by carefully packing it in Carl Rungius' baggage when he returned to New York. Once the head was mounted the question of its sale could be dealt with. Since Jimmy knew that a fake world's record had recently sold for $1,500, he decided to put a high price on it, a fact witnessed by Clark's letter to him in early 1922:

This is some sheep head! And you ask some price. I hope you get it for your own good, and whoever pays that will certainly appreciate it all the more. From what I know of the business, I doubt you will get half the price, but there is certainly no harm in trying.

It certainly is a wonder, and it hardly seems possible that a head surpassing this one shall ever be obtained, and I think the party who eventually gets it will always be able to claim a world's record.

Although Clark tried, he was not able to find a customer for the figure Jimmy was asking. He did keep up his contact though, finding Jimmy several hunting customers during the twenties, and Jimmy secured him a number of other good heads for his customers. In addition to his skill as a taxidermist, Clark was one of the foremost bronze sculptors of the day, and in return for one or two trophy heads Jimmy was able to add a beautiful Clark caribou bronze to his wildlife art collection. As to the record sheep, it was eventually sold to Dr. Henry Beck, a collector of trophy heads in New York, who paid several thousand dollars for it. Beck kept it in his personal collection for a number of years and then donated it to the American Museum of Natural History in New York, where it became the centre attraction in the bighorn sheep exhibit.

Jimmy's actions with respect to the sale of the record sheep head and his relationship with Clark were entirely consistent with his point of view at this time. He had sold good game heads and, on occasion, whole animals to collectors before, often to scientific organizations or institutions, and the record ram's head was regarded as simply another item of stock-in-trade, albeit an extremely valuable one. Of course, it was also important from a promotional point-of-view, and it was not long before a photograph of the head was adorning his business stationery and advertising material.

At the same time as he was experiencing his crowning achievement in the hunting line, Jimmy's relationship with his old clientele was changing. McAleenan and his companions Brooks, Murgatroyd and Frothingham made a trip in the fall of 1921 and during it Jimmy and his old friend had a strong difference of opinion. A mutual friend wrote, "I am sorry to hear that your trip with the McAleenan outfit left a bad taste," and in his last letter to Jimmy, McAleenan offered to make up but at the same time referred to "the sullen and don't give a damn periods that come to you at times." Dr. Brooks returned in 1923 for a hunt and a stay at Bow Lake, which he referred to as "Belmont on the Bow," and afterward he wrote to thank Jimmy for the wonderful trip. Tragically, the next time he heard from Brooks it was a letter informing him that McAleenan had been killed in a fall from the roof of his house. Brooks predicted that "this is probably the end of all our hunting trips."

Despite the loss of this important group of clients, Jimmy still had as many hunting parties as he could handle, and he could now offer them an even more diverse game bag than he could provide his earlier customers. Up until the end of the First World War, two varieties of game eagerly sought by hunters, moose and elk, could not be found in the Canadian Rockies. Although both were native species, their numbers had dwindled in the period before Jimmy had arrived in Banff and, according to him, because of the depredations of the Indians they eventually disappeared altogether. Jimmy recalled that moose began to show up again about 1908 or 1910, when they began drifting back in from British Columbia. A few years later, in 1917, the government reintroduced elk by shipping in some excess animals from a herd in Yellowstone Park. By the twenties both had established themselves in sufficient numbers to allow them to be hunted again.

In the early twenties, many new sportsmen were taken out, and several of them would become return customers. Among them were Henry J. Munger, president of the Lewis M. Weed Clothing Company in New York; Clement Wood, a Philadelphia attorney; Dr. Brace Paddock of Pittsfield, Massachusetts; and Thomas W. Berger, head of The Deft Devices Company in Philadelphia. But the hunting party that Jimmy would remember best in later years was one composed of James T. Wilson, vice-president of the Nash Motor Company, his brother Don Wilson, president of Nash-Utica Motors and their friend C. C. Allen. The story of how he came to take these men out was typical of the value of his wide connections at this time.

At some point Jimmy had made the acquaintance of the colourful creator and promoter of the Calgary Stampede, Guy Weadick. Jimmy periodically entered some of his men in the annual Stampede packing contest and Weadick kept in touch with him about this, as well as using some of his horses in Stampede events. By the mid-twenties Weadick had begun promoting the ranch he owned on the Highwood River as a dude ranch operation, but he admitted to Jimmy in a letter that "I have really neglected going after much business for my ranch in the manner I should have, owing to the fact that I have been devoting most of my time the year around to exploiting 'The Stampede'." In an effort to improve on this situation he asked Jimmy to help out: "I will mail you shortly a rate card and also a few folders and at any time you can advise anyone regarding our place I will appreciate it, and you can rest assured that at any time I can turn anyone to you, I will gladly do so." This appealed to Jimmy and the two exchanged the names of several customers. In April, 1925, Weadick suggested Jimmy write to Charles Nash, the president of Nash Motors in Kenosha, Wisconsin to see if he could interest him in a hunting trip.

Jimmy acted on the suggestion and although Nash responded that he could not contemplate a trip at the time, having recently returned from hunting the Cassiar region of B.C., he said he would put some friends in touch. The friends turned out to be his son-in-law James Wilson and his brother Don. Although they did not respond to his offer immediately, in early 1927 James Wilson paid a visit to Carl Rungius' studio and then wrote Jimmy stating that "he spoke of you very highly" and asking him to quote on a trip for the following fall. A booking was soon made and Wilson quickly began to lay out some of his requirements for the trip, including the use of a tent instead of the usual tepee, the provision of folding chairs and cots, a request for Jimmy to pressure the government into raising bag limits, and, above all, a good supply of Scotch. At the last moment Wilson was forced to cancel, and the outing was postponed until the fall of 1928. When it did take place the Wilsons were joined by their friend C. C. Allen and everyone succeeded in getting the bighorn sheep they were after. James Wilson had his mounted by James Clark and wrote to say "it looks so good the Mrs. is going to allow me to put it up in the Library." Like so many others, he also stated that the experience had been one of the best of their lives and that he would be pleased to help line up other prospective parties.

The Wilsons were not the only party that Jimmy's working relationship with Weadick gained him. Several pleasure parties, an equally important part of his business, were also lined up. In July, 1925 Mrs. Frederick Longfellow of New York and seven members of her family went on a camping trip with Jimmy after a stay at Weadick's ranch. Jimmy was able to respond in kind when he arranged for some of his best pleasure trip customers, the family of New York real estate magnate Joseph P. Day and their friends Arlene Voorhies, Augusta Ely and Annie Call, to visit Weadick's ranch.

While hunters and pleasure parties remained Jimmy's bread and butter during the hectic twenties, it was a new group of customers that provided the most interesting trips. These were mountaineers, a type of client that he had heard very little from since the years immediately after the turn of the century. With them he would make a number of noteworthy climbs of his own, adding another chapter to the growing Simpson legend.

An alpinist who would make several trips with Jimmy in the twenties and who would provide him with many other mountaineering contacts was Dr. J. Monroe Thorington of Philadelphia. Thorington was a successful opthamologist who had climbed a good deal in Europe by the time he first contacted Jimmy in 1921, and he would establish a fine reputation as a Canadian Rockies explorer and mountaineer in the years thereafter. A man keenly interested in alpine history, as well as his own place in that history, Thorington probably first encountered Jimmy's name in the accounts of Sir James Outram's climbs in the Mount Columbia area in 1902. In May, 1921 he wrote and inquired about the rates for two or three persons for a three week trip to the region around Mount Forbes. Jimmy responded with a quote of $900 for two or $1,100 for three, and, reminding Thorington that "I was in there years ago with James Outram & Dr. J. Norman Collie when they made the first ascent of Mount Forbes," stated that "if twenty-two years' experience count for anything I ought not to fail at my end."

The trip did not materialize until the next year and the party consisted of Thorington, fellow-alpinist Howard Palmer and Swiss guide Edward Feuz, Jr. The destination was the Freshfield Group, near the headwaters of the main branch of the North Saskatchewan River and, as the best approach was by way of Howse Pass, the pack train of seventeen horses left from Field with Jimmy guiding, Tommy Frayne as cook and Bill

Baptie and Mousie Saddington as packer and horse wrangler. As they proceeded by way of the Amiskwi River and Pass, the going proved tough because of the downed timber, which Thorington described as "piled up and interlaced like gigantic jackstraws." His wisdom in choosing his guide immediately became apparent because "Jim would be off his horse — he was in the lead — making the chips fly and the woods resound with the echo of his chopping." This was just one of many times Jimmy would prove himself during the trip by providing first hand knowledge of the geography and routes in the neighbourhood of Mount Freshfield and forming the line of supply to the climbers while they were engaged in their mountaineering pursuits. For example, while Thorington and Feuz explored the peaks surrounding the Freshfield Icefield from a high camp, "Jim had packed bread — and an occasional ptarmigan — up to the high camp for us." When they left the area, the party had bagged six peaks over 10,000 feet in elevation and Thorington pronounced it "a most satisfactory and interesting trip" and admitted that "we were more lucky than usual as far as the climbing went."

These results, and Jimmy's stories of the mountains further north around Mount Columbia, led Thorington to plan another outing the following year and he wrote "our outfitter, of course, would be no other than Jim Simpson." This time the doctor was to be accompanied by a fellow medical man, Dr. William Ladd, a specialist in the treatment of diabetes at the Presbyterian Hospital in New York. Feuz was not available to the party, and the trip was almost cancelled before Jimmy came up with a replacement, his friend the Austrian climbing guide Conrad Kain, who he described as "perhaps the best guide that has ever been in the country for any length of time." The team was completed by LaCasse and Frayne and the party departed the old schoolhouse at Lake Louise, which Jimmy had been able to rent from the CPR as a headquarters, on July 27th.

Passing Bow Lake, Thorington commented on Jimmy's camp, "a snug boat-house on the sandy beach and a regular block-house of logs where one could spend the most restful sort of vacation." They made their way by the usual route up the North Fork to the Alexandra River valley and followed the trail Jimmy had used on the trip with Outram towards the mountains at its head. Bad weather limited the mountaineering at first and the party had to content itself with exploring the Alexandra Glacier and the trail up the Castleguard River. While they were doing so, an amusing incident occurred that showed the degree to which Jimmy lost track of time while out on the trail:

It must have been about this time that Jim, apropos of nothing in particular, remarked that his birthday was about to recur. Tommy and I made secret plans. When the day arrived, Tommy concocted a gigantic doughnut, liberally powdered with sugar and mounted on a pedestal of heather. We stood the candle from our folding-lantern in the centre and the result was almost artistic. At lunch-time it was brought in with all ceremony and presented to "Chief Nashan" . . . Jim was much surprised; but we were still more so, when he confessed that although the date was right he had been a whole month short on time!

The event would become the subject of many a good laugh between Jimmy and his friend "Doc" over the course of their fifty-year friendship.

Thorington's party camped in the meadows below Mount Castleguard, a spot he described as a "wranglers dream" because of its abundance of water, wood and horse feed, and above all because "the horses can't get away!" From an alpinist's point of view it was an ideal place to attack some of the great peaks of the Columbia Icefield, and it was not long before the entire group, including Jimmy, LaCasse and Frayne, were doing just that. On July 6th they climbed nearby Mount Castleguard in four hours, from whence tremendous views of the Columbia Icefield were achieved, and took advantage of the opportunity to plan the routes for further climbs. But, according to Thorington, Jimmy and Conrad, who was also an inveterate trapper, were distracted by a different objective: "Jim and Conrad are lying flat on the shale, with a map spread out; there is a great pointing of fingers toward distant valleys, and the remarks which come to my ears indicate that fur-bearing animals next trapping season had best look out for themselves."

Although the ascent of Castleguard was not difficult, it was the only recorded climb Jimmy had made since his days with the Topographic Survey. The experience seemed to re-kindle his long surpressed interest in Mount Columbia, the first ascent of which Outram had denied him the opportunity to participate in 21 years before. In any event, when Thorington, Ladd, and Kain set out to try the second ascent on July 14th, Jimmy was the fourth on the rope. It would be the highlight of his alpine career:

Even from the level of the icefield, at 10,000 feet, Columbia merits its proud position as the second elevation of the chain. It had seemed so far above our heads when we were on Castleguard, we wondered if we should ever reach it. But on July 14th we started out. The climbing party derived added pleasure from the presence of Simpson; Jim had been with Sir James Outram and the guide Christian Kaufmann, but had not climbed, at the time of the first-ascent, in 1902, just twenty-one years before. Reaching Castleguard shoulder (3.50-5.30 A. M.), we found the snow in fine condition and rapidly traversed the tracks made some days previously.

Morning sun was gilding the ranges; the wind blew forcefully, and we turned toward Columbia, gleaming in the ice-blue of clear weather distance. Insects innumerable are carried up onto the ice by air currents from the British Columbia side; and at 10,000 feet and above, we collected moths and beetles of many varieties. . .

Although favorable conditions of snow made travel more easy than our tour de force to The Twins, we again had to cross many gaps and deceptive, crevassed hollows. Far out on the icefield, shortly after ten o'clock, we had lunch on the flat snow above the head of Columbia Glacier. . .

We were soon at the bergschrund, a narrow chasm easily crossed, and on steeper snow beyond. At 11,000 feet we halted by a rocky outcrop where water trickled; we were in the centre of and more than half way up the great eastern snow-face, practically treading the Continental Divide. We wondered what the other outfitters would have said if they could have seen Jim with an ice-axe, roped in a climbing party? The pitch steepened; steps were occasionally cut; a stinging relentless wind tore up the snow-crust until the air seemed full of whirling white shingles. We toiled upward for some time in the gale, in some danger of having snow-glasses broken by bits of flying ice. Traversing slightly to the north, we were more sheltered, and, cutting through a narrow bit of cornice, soon were shaking hands on the summit. . .

Forty minutes we spent on the summit, and fifteen more, out of the wind, on a level spot below the cornice. The top of Gamma! Let no one think that Columbia is a mere snow-hump rising from a neve; it is a distinct peak in every sense, looking its height and quite worthy of its place. Simpson intends to climb it every twenty-one years from now on!

Seemingly enamoured with his own feats on snow and ice, Jimmy decided to put his pack train through the same paces by taking them down the Saskatchewan Glacier shortly after returning to camp. According to Thorington, the reason for this was that "for many years there had existed, among the outfitters, the desire to find a direct route practicable for horses between the heads of the Castleguard and Sunwapta River," to shorten transportation time. Jimmy had scouted out the possibilities and had come to the conclusion that the most direct route, over the icefield, would be difficult but possible. The crossing began at a small marginal lake beside the Saskatchewan Glacier and nearly opposite Mount Athabasca:

A shore of flat moraine permitted the pack-train to progress to level ice. Our horses on the glacier made an unusual procession; but, at first timid, they soon became accustomed to their surroundings and, like true mountaineers, hopped over the little cracks and crevasses. It was necessary, in avoiding a lateral glacier entering from the south, to take to the central ice for a short distance. The horses were taken down the glacier for more than four miles, with devious winding around the large transverse crevasses. The steep terminal moraine, with treacherously balanced boulders and slippery glacial mud, was most troublesome, requiring some trail-building and considerable care to avoid damage to the pack-train. But before evening the last horse was safely off and camp finally made below the tongue on the flats toward the south side near a pleasant waterfall.

This first crossing of the Saskatchewan Glacier with a pack train would win Jimmy tremendous admiration in outfitting and guiding circles and, coming as it did only two days after his ascent of Mount Columbia, a notable achievement in the mountaineering world, it would add immeasurably to his already considerable mystique.

The feat marked the completion of Thorington and Ladd's 1923 expedition and on returning home the latter wrote "I don't think we could have possibly had the success we did without your wise judgement in picking the moving time, and getting us across the river, and so many of the little things that count in making a trip go well." Thorington paid his tribute in a slightly different way. After a trip with Jasper outfitter Curly Phillips to the mountains around the Whirlpool River in 1924, he began writing a book to recount his Rocky Mountain experiences. Published in 1925 under the title *The Glittering Mountains of Canada*, its dedication read, "To My Guides Edward Feuz Jr., Conrad Kain, James Simpson With The Affection Which Has Grown From Mutual Understanding And Respect In Days On The Heights And By The Campfires Of The Northland." In the introduction was the equally glowing remark that in 1922 and 1923 the pack trains "were in charge of James Simpson, a pioneer and hunter of wide experience, a powerful mountaineer, a man of resource and initiative, and withal, a true friend."

Thorington would return to Jimmy's door in 1926 and 1933 for further climbing expeditions and, like Outram's before it, his book would provide a useful advertisement for the services his outfitter was capable of offering the mountaineering fraternity. But Thorington, who made a point of knowing everyone doing alpine work anywhere, went further, reinforcing the value of the book by personally marketing Jimmy's abilities to these people. One of the most interesting of the groups he influenced would hire Jimmy to guide a trip to Jasper, an area he had very little familiarity with.

In later life, when questioned by Thorington about his trips to the north of the Columbia Icefield, Jimmy would respond, "Frankly, the country is so damn big that the Jasper region those days seemed to be 'the outer rim of the back of beyond,' that weeks were needed to get there & with only cayuses to do it on it seemed a fantasy." Despite the psychological barrier its remoteness engendered, he recalled that he made three or four trips to Jasper during his career, the first with a party of sixteen girls and the second with three men from Philadelphia arranged by Thorington in 1925. The three were H. E. Sibson and Samuel Felix, both involved in manufacturing businesses, and E. S. Higgins, vice-president and general manager of the Yellow Cab Co. of Philadelphia. Although only two had any trail experience at all, an evening viewing Thorington's pictures got them interested in visiting some of the same country he had recently traversed and then carrying right on through to Jasper. In May, Thorington wrote Jimmy that "after some wrestling I have succeeded in inducing Messrs. Sibson, Felix and Higgins to wire you and accept terms for the August trip, Louise to Jasper."

The trip took place in August and its early stages consisted of a duplication of some of the feats of Thorington's outing of 1923, including an ascent of Mount Castleguard and a pack train traverse of the Saskatchewan Glacier. From there the party proceeded into Jimmy's Brazeau territory, then over Jonas Pass to Maligne Pass and down the Maligne River to Maligne Lake, and, after a layover, down the Maligne past Medicine Lake and the Maligne Canyon to Jasper Park Lodge. Thorington had also made arrangements for Jimmy to meet the party of Allan H. Reed, manager of the Curtis Publishing Company, in Jasper so he could bring it back to Lake Louise over roughly the same route. Reed cancelled at the last moment so, instead of a leisurely three week return journey, Jimmy's men deadheaded straight through and reached home in 12 days. As Jimmy's profit had been predicated on parties going both ways, Reed made up the loss to him and later took several enjoyable trips under his guidance. Almost all the clients who had to cancel with Jimmy from time to time did likewise, and he rarely found himself too much out of pocket from these annoying occurrences.

As for the Sibson party, they all wrote Jimmy to say how much they enjoyed their trip and how healthy they felt as a result of it. Jimmy, in reporting to Thorington, agreed about the good time but wasn't so sure about the health:

Messrs. Sibson & friends had a good time in every way. I had them down the icefield as we went & also up Castleguard, but that was an effort I did not think they would make. Felix took his pulse quite often on the climb & was surprised as hell when he couldn't find mine at all. Perhaps I fed

*them too much moose meat & their wind got short, but it was long
enough when Tommy called "Come & get it."*

Perhaps the most active alpinist Thorington helped to attract as a client
for Jimmy was a young Harvard student named Dyson Duncan, whose
acquaintance would lead to another significant mountaineering feat.
Duncan wrote to Jimmy in May, 1926 that "you have been recom-
mended to us by four separate parties who have been out with you
personally, and they praise your skill as a guide." Among the four were
Thorington and Henry Emerson Tuttle, the art professor at Groton
School, Massachusetts from which Duncan and three fellow students
wanting a trip had just graduated. Their outing that year was confined
to fishing and a bit of hunting in the Red Deer and Clearwater River
areas, but when Duncan returned in 1927 with fellow student Twining
Lynes it was with the intention of doing some climbing. The object of
their attention on their three week outing was the now-popular Freshfield
Group, and in particular peak number four on Mount Lyell, which was
unclimbed.

The 20 horse pack train set out from Lake Louise with Jimmy in the
lead at the end of June, taking the usual route up the Bow Valley and then
up to the headwaters of the Saskatchewan near Glacier Lake. Just as they
arrived bad weather set in and the eager climbers had to cool their heels
in camp for four days "listening to the intermittent patter of raindrops
and hailstones on the canvas of the tepee." This was necessary because,
as their Swiss guide Ernest Feuz put it: "Ya-a! De Gott damn glowds dey
keep pooshing up from de Selkurks. Iss no gude to climb: up on de
snowfields it blizzes und it rizzles." Finally the weather cleared and it
turned colder, allowing the four-member party to set out for the long
trek to the nearly inaccessible Lyell 4. This required an afternoon trek
over the East Lyell Glacier and a night on the lateral moraine during
which they "smoked and chatted" around a blazing campfire. The next
day, July 8th, they set out at 3 a.m., and they found the snow so heavy
that one of the party fell into the crevasse between the bergschrund and
the slopes of the peak proper and was only saved from harm by the rope.
From there it was a long grind up the ridge, with another near disaster
occuring just as the summit was neared. The summit ridge held a huge

overhanging cornice and when Feuz stuck in his ice axe a big piece of cornice several yards square fractured off, leaving the climbers "standing on a ridgepole where a moment before there had been a regular sidewalk." This left an insecure knob just big enough for two people, a misfortune that denied Jimmy the summit: "I did not make the last 20 feet as there was only room for two with safety on the narrow mushroomed top. Ernest let three make it but there was no use holding up the party & unroping just for me to go the last 20 feet so I unroped at the tail end & the rest did it." By the time the climbers had made their way back down to base camp they had been out for 30 hours without sleep or shelter.

After their first ascent on Lyell 4, Duncan and Lynes expressed an interest in taking on Mount Columbia and Jimmy delivered them to its base. Its ascent proved as arduous as that of Lyell 4, taking 31 hours, but, as Jimmy wrote Thorington, "I did not go on that jaunt." Nevertheless, he jokingly promised "in 17 more years I will — just to fulfill your prediction." On the return trip to Lake Louise, though, he did participate in the ascent of Mount Wilson.

The culmination of Jimmy's mountaineering career came nearby and shortly thereafter. Returning with Duncan's party to Lake Louise, he immediately left with another group headed by Alfred Castle, one of his most important customers. Castle was a senior attorney with Castle and Cook of Honolulu, Hawaii and a member of the family that owned the Hawaiian Pineapple (Dole) Company. He had begun his visits to the Rockies as a young boy in 1895 and he would ultimately go out on the trail and visit Jimmy at his lodge a total of 15 times. They first met at Bow Lake in 1921 when Castle and pioneer mountaineer Walter Wilcox camped near Jimmy on a trip to try to gain access to the little known Valley of the Hidden Lakes at the head of the Red Deer River, an area they had reconnoitred five years previously. This trip resulted in the first thorough exploration of the valley and the naming of three lakes, Gwendolyn, Donald and Alfred, after Castle's children. In 1925 Castle asked Jimmy to outfit and guide he and two of his three children to view the lakes that bore their names, and he was very satisfied with the service. Therefore, when he returned for a climb of Mount Columbia in 1927 accompanied by his son Alfred, his friend J. H. Barnes and the

Swiss guide Rudolph Aemmer, he once more requested Jimmy's help.

Castle's favourite recollection of the trip in later years focussed on Jimmy's wonderful ability with the horses. He recalled that after the party had crossed the swollen Saskatchewan River late in the afternoon, they stopped to make camp and the unattended horses quickly swam back to an island, and were making longing glances in the direction of Bow Lake. The water level was so high that it was dangerous for Jimmy to go after them, so he attempted to talk them back: "Jim quickly got on a point where he could look across at them and began to talk in a friendly and persuasive tone. He finally got the attention of his pet saddle horse, Cappy, and persuaded him to swim back to the north side of the river. The others followed him." Saved from a long walk back to Bow Lake, the group proceeded on to Mount Columbia and made its ascent. It was the third time in a matter of five years that a Simpson party had achieved success on the peak. They then turned back towards the Saskatchewan and, when they reached their former camping spot, Jimmy made the momentous announcement that it was his 50th birthday. This time he was not out on the date, and after the cook had whipped up a large bunch of wild strawberries that Castle painstakingly picked, they all celebrated with the best strawberry cake any of them had ever tasted.

Within a few days of celebrating this landmark in his life, Jimmy was nearly convinced that it would be his last. The occasion was the ascent of Mount Cline in the Saskatchewan Valley near Mount Wilson, which Aemmer had suggested they climb as it was the only remaining first ascent over 11,000 feet in the area. Figuring out the proper approach took several days, after which the ascent proved quite straightforward until the ridge leading to the summit was gained. Jimmy later described the experience:

We had Rudolph Aemmer as a guide and we were travelling this narrow ridge. It's cut in three places going along the ridge before you make the peak, and the last cut is the worst. Rudolph took a look at it and he said, "I think we can make this." The ridge isn't any more than twelve feet wide and in the last cut there is a big rock stuck in it which Rudolph called a keystone. I saw him go down. I was right behind him on the rope. Castle came up as he started down and had a look at him and he said to me, "Do you want to die this sudden." It was a thousand feet down on either side — absolutely nothing — and all overhanging. I said, "I don't feel quite like it." He said, "Well, we'll see what this damn fool guide does."

I saw Rudolph go down and he got on the keystone. He stuck his axe in his belt, a sign it is going to be tough because he wants both his hands. I saw him work his way up the cliff on the other side. When he was nearly at the top of the other side, he found his left foot where his right foot should be. I saw him feel the rock with his hands and then this darn fool hung by his fingers and changed his feet. I saw every knuckle turn snow white. I thought, "My God, if he falls will this rope hold." He put his right foot on it and his left up a little higher and went up on top and said, "Come on, it is all right." I went next.

This was the last ascent of the expedition, as well as the last major recorded climb of Jimmy's life. At 50, it was time to think of keeping his hide intact for the next half century.

CHAPTER NINE

The Simpsons of Banff

During the same period as his outfitting and guiding business was reaching its apogee and he was beginning development at Bow Lake, Jimmy was busy on the home front with his growing family and community involvements. Equally so Billie, and with the active participation of their children in sports as they grew up, the Simpsons were soon regarded as one of Banff's most involved and community-minded families. Even at that, both Jimmy and Billie found time to pursue their own particular interests and hobbies during these busy years, and both made strides that resulted in more fulfilling lives.

Although the raising of the children fell largely on her shoulders, Billie was determined not to let her fine mind languish. Given her father's horticultural background, it was not surprising that she should be interested in flowers and gardening, and on the few occasions she did get the opportunity to go out with Jimmy she began to develop a lifelong interest in alpine botany. At home, she was an avid reader, and she found time in her schedule to keep pace with her husband's growing library, particularly in the field of exploration literature. But she also indulged her love of the classics when the opportunity arose, and with some other ladies in town worked hard to provide an artistic outlet for the dramatic talents of those in the community. In 1924, under the leadership of Mrs. Margaret Greenham, the operator of Banff's private "Mountain School," she helped form the Banff Literary-Dramatic Club with the initial objective of studying Irish drama. During its first year, she and two other Banff ladies, Mrs. Kennedy and Mrs. Robinson, toiled diligently and were able to produce three one-act plays in the Simpson's living room. These were the first of many such productions, thereafter held in the Lux Theatre, and with the addition of other related activities, such as dramatic readings and discussions, the club would become the primary manifestation of Banff culture for the next quarter century. As one of its pillars, Billie would be one of only three members involved from beginning to end.

Figure skating was the other great passion that Billie began to develop in these years. Seeing "The Great Charlotte" in New York had moved her deeply, and when she settled in Banff she took every opportunity to learn about this beautiful sport that fit so well with her artistic and dramatic impulses. There were a few books on the subject, which she eagerly sought out, and there was one man in Banff, George Paris, who had learned the basics of figure skating and owned the proper skates. She began by learning from him, skating on the ice of Vermilion Lakes when it was bare or on the community rink that was cleared on the river in front of the Simpson home. As her skills improved, she also periodically received assistance from Eileen "Bunty" Noble, the first champion of the Calgary Glencoe Club, who would often come up to Banff to skate. Soon she would be on the ice almost daily, pushing the baby sleigh in front of her, and Jimmy was moved to build his own rink in the yard for fear of the river ice.

By the mid-twenties, Billie had gained sufficient confidence and ability to begin instructing some of Banff's youngsters. Her prime pupils were her own two daughters, Margaret and Mary, who were accomplished skaters before they even started school. As an outlet for her pupils' talents, she began to get them involved in the Banff Winter Carnival, an annual winter sports event that attracted competitors from all over western Canada and the northwestern United States. Billie helped to organize the "art skating" competition, matching her husband's volunteer efforts on the carnival 's executive committee and as organizer of the annual bonspeil associated with it.

Apart from winter sports, Jimmy had little time to match "the Madam's" involvement in groups and organizations because of the nature of his occupation, which kept him away from home for long periods over much of the year. He made an exception for organizations that promoted his business interests, two of which emerged during the twenties. One was the Rocky Mountain Outfitters' (later Guides') Association, which was formed in May, 1922 as a result of abuses in the business arising from the growing level of competition. Jimmy was one of the eleven outfitting concerns who initially supported the Association's objective "to have one official body who will be empowered to negotiate with the dominion and provincial governments in all matters pertaining to the outfitting business throughout the Rocky Mountains, such as the inter-provincial recognition of guides' licenses, betterment of trails in the park, game and fishing regulations etc." But he quickly came to the conclusion that the organization was simply a mouthpiece for the Brewster company and later that year he wrote to the Superintendent resigning from it, stating that "in future any applications or suggestions from myself will be from an independent individual connected with the outfitting business." Another, more successful, relationship with an organization helping to benefit outfitters soon replaced it when he became a charter member of the CPR-sponsored Trail Riders of the Canadian Rockies in 1924.

Jimmy's love-hate relationship with the CPR, first evident when he visited New York, had continued on into the twenties. At the same time as he depended on the company to provide him favours, including transportation, advertising and a headquarters at Lake Louise, he resented the concession system that gave the bulk of CPR business to the Brewster company. Several times in the late teens and early twenties, when the Brewsters were experiencing difficulties, he approached the railway about taking over the concession, and he was always disappointed by their refusal. When he did manage to attract some of their business, such as a 1920 film-making trip on bighorn sheep with Banff photographer Byron Harmon performed at John Murray Gibbon's specific request, he responded by submitting what Gibbon regarded as an outrageous bill. Nevertheless, there was a grudging respect by each party for the other's point of view, and Jimmy often put forward ideas that he thought would benefit both of them. His position on the changes to the parks boundaries affecting his Brazeau sheep-hunting range was one. This he tied in with the need for the CPR to wake up to the value of the area north of Lake Louise from a tourist perspective, particularly since the rival Grand Trunk Pacific Railway had started to promote tourism in Jasper Park north of the Columbia Icefield. Eventually, Allan Seymour, General Tourist Agent for the CPR, recognized the value of what Jimmy was preaching and took some steps to rectify the company's almost total neglect of promotion and development opportunities in the area.

The CPR's recognition of Jimmy's talents and personal popularity with many visitors to the Rockies led Gibbon to ask him to take a leading role in the Trail Riders. As General Publicity Agent for the CPR and an avid rider himself, Gibbon had initiated the idea for an organization sponsoring trail riding in 1923 and he soon began discussing it with his numerous contacts in the mountains. He proposed that the organization take the form of an "Order," wherein badges of various grades would be awarded to those riding from 50 to 2,500 miles of mountain trails. The focus of its activities would be an annual Trail Riders camp and ride, somewhat like the Alpine Club of Canada's annual camp, during which those in attendance would go on a three day or longer ride over a different pre-selected route every year. All the outfitting and guiding would be placed in the hands of the Rocky Mountain Guides' Association, providing they gave the most competitive rates.

Although no longer a member of the Association, and therefore not eligible to handle any of the rides, Jimmy could see the value of such an organization for the promotion of his business. Because the automobile was beginning to make a strong incursion into Banff park, with many more tourists now seeing the sights from touring cars and the first sightseeing buses rather than the back of a horse, it was obvious that an organization backed by the CPR, with its wide advertising and promotional resources, was needed if pleasure riding were going to survive. Thus when Gibbon approached him about being one of the members of the organizing committee for the Trail Riders, along with former guides Tom Wilson and Jim and Bill Brewster, Jimmy agreed.

Gibbon forwarded him the draft constitution and by-laws for comment and Jimmy pointed out that if the organization were going to be taken seriously it had to be very strict on awarding the various grades of buttons. Gibbon concurred and suggested that "if the Membership Committee is confined strictly to professional guides this ideal will be maintained." Consequently, when the organization officially came into existence in June, 1924, Jimmy found himself on both the executive committee and the membership committee.

His fears about the awarding of buttons were apparently realized during the first annual trail ride in the Yoho Valley. In response to a letter from Jimmy in September, 1924, Gibbon admitted that "a certain number of buttons were undoubtedly given out on the personal assurance of guides and on written lists of trails ridden, which were measured up by Phil Moore and Jim Brewster." As to why he was not consulted as a member of the committee, Gibbon offered that "you were away so much and they probably did not wish to lose the members by delay."

The Trail Riders organization immediately proved popular and its activities were expanded every year thereafter. By 1929 its membership was over 1,500, with a considerable number of them holding the 2,500 mile badge. Its ability to influence the government led Jimmy to overlook some of his concerns, and he remained active on the executive committee until 1926 and on the membership committee until 1927, after which he served for several years on its council. Likewise, Billie, who preferred hiking to riding, served a year as president of its sister organization, the Sky Line Trail Hikers of the Canadian Rockies.

Even though Jimmy was asked to bid on outfitting the Trail Riders on several occasions after the rules on the guides' association monopoly were relaxed, he decided not to become directly involved. Instead, he continued to make his opinion on matters affecting his business in the park known as an individual and through his political contacts. These latter were considerable and accounted for his only other official organizational involvement during these years. His political loyalties went back to the Simpson family's ties with the Conservative party in England, although as a young lad bent on raising hell he certainly had not taken any great interest in them at that time. Soon after arriving in Canada, though, he had an experience that confirmed his family's party outlook:

Six weeks after I was in Canada and I was at Laggan there was an election on. The deputy returning officer was a strong Liberal and he said, "You're going to be my poll clerk and you're going to vote." I said, "I haven't got a vote because I haven't been in the country long enough and I'm not of voting age." "Never mind," he said, "you're going to vote." He opened a ballot and he said, "You're going to put your x right there." I said, "Is he Liberal or Conservative?" "Never mind, never mind, it don't matter a damn bit," he said, "put your cross right there." It was supposed to be a secret ballot but when I came back from the polling booth he opened it up and looked at it and said, "That's correct," and then folded it back up and put it in the ballot box. "God Almighty," I said to myself, "I think I'll stay Conservative."

Although he was a Conservative supporter earlier, Jimmy did not really become actively involved in politics until about 1915. He was well acquainted with R. B. Bennett, a partner of Senator James Lougheed's in one of Calgary's major law firms, and Member of Parliament for Calgary East. As Bennett was one of the most influential members in Alberta, Jimmy often spoke and wrote to him about conditions at Banff, in particular about the government officials who held sway in the Parks Branch. Bennett listened and in 1917 promised action as soon as war conditions allowed: "I am very much impressed by the statement you made in your letter regarding conditions. I cannot persuade the official at this moment to deal with them but I promise you that if I live I will have them investigated before this summer is out, and if the facts are anything like what you think they are, there is going to be a very great "house cleaning" in Banff. I know what conditions were like there once and I do not propose that they shall be repeated if I can help it." To Jimmy's distress, Bennett decided not to run in the election of 1917, as he expected to be appointed to the Senate, and his influence on local issues waned. Bennett ran for the seat of Calgary West, which included Banff, in the election of 1921, and was defeated, but when he stood for the 1925 election Jimmy and other local Conservative stalwarts, such as Billy Mather and William Warren, worked hard at making sure he wouldn't be defeated again. The evidence of their efforts showed in the election results — out of 995 eligible voters in Banff, 864 voted and 585 ballots were cast for Bennett. A few days after the election, he wrote a letter to Jimmy and Billie thanking them for their telegram of congratulations and the work that they had done on his behalf.

With Bennett in Ottawa, Jimmy had a ready ear for his point of view on a variety of issues affecting the park, and he did not hesitate to make use of the opportunity. Bennett's influence grew even stronger when he became the Minister of Finance in 1926 and then head of the Conservative party and Leader of the Opposition in 1927. Grateful for his support, Bennett helped Jimmy where he could. When they met, he often asked Jimmy if he would be interested in a government position, arguing, "Now quit this going outdoors — you've got a brain in your head and you'll go up the ladder quickly." Jimmy typically responded: "R. B., I can't do it. I've mixed with every kind of hobo, mixed with second storey men, and mixed with train robbers, but I've got to draw the line somewhere. I can't take your government job." Bennett would laugh and reply, "Jimmy, your hopeless."

When Bennett became Prime Minister in 1930 he was preoccupied with battling the onslaught of the Depression, but tried to do the best he could for the constituency. Jimmy claimed that Banff Avenue would never have been rebuilt except for the fact that one day when he was with Bennett and they were crossing the street Bennett lost his rubber in the mud and fumed, "I'm going to have this damn street paved." Despite their usual good relationship, both men were strong willed and sometimes locked horns. On one occasion, Bennett took great offence to a note taking him to task for not acknowledging Jimmy when they passed on the street in Calgary. And Jimmy admitted that he had even voted against Bennett on one occasion "because we got in an argument and I told him he was too damn dictatorial."

Apart from his active involvement in local sports and these few other public activities, most of Jimmy's spare time was spent pursuing his personal interests and hobbies. These were extensive and reflected his multi-faceted personality. Of course, one of his earliest consuming passions, and one that he continued to expand on, was art collecting. As always, wildlife played an important role in this interest and he usually found some way to fulfill his current desires through his business activities, such as with the major additions to his bird painting collection in the twenties.

One of the first artists with whom Jimmy had come in contact was the noted American ornithological painter Louis Agassiz Fuertes of Ithaca, New York. Fuertes was closely associated with William Hornaday and other members of the Boone and Crockett Club and often worked on birds in cooperation with scientific institutions. In 1907 he accompanied

Frank Chapman, Associate Curator of the American Museum of Natural History, to the Rockies to make a collection of alpine birds. Jimmy assisted them and in appreciation Fuertes painted him a picture of a rosy finch with Mount Temple near Lake Louise as a background, inscribing it "To Mr. James Simpson with the regards of Louis Agassiz Fuertes April 1909." The painting became one of the foundations of Jimmy's art collection and over the years he periodically kept in touch with Fuertes, but it was not until 1921 that he was able to add a companion piece. This came about as a result of Fuertes' request that Jimmy find him a pair of mule deer horns and a pair of elk horns to use in modelling for some animal pictures that he was attempting. Not only did Jimmy agree to do this, but he also insisted on sending the artist a pair of sheep horns as well. Fuertes was delighted and wrote suggesting that if Jimmy would not take payment "at least let me know what you'd like a picture of, so that I can feel at least decent in accepting these things." Further correspondence resulted in Fuertes agreeing to paint a picture of a blue jay Jimmy had in mind and, in May, 1921 he wrote "just a line to tell you that your blue jay is on his flight, bringing his apple blossoms with him" and expressing the hope that it would fit well with the rest of Jimmy's collection.

Similar arrangements with other artists brought Jimmy equally treasured prizes. In 1920 he was asked by the noted British bird illustrator Archibald Thorburn to gather some bird skins from the Rockies and ship them to England in return for a fee. He did so and used the money to order two Thorburn sketches. Later, in 1923, in return for a continuing supply of material, Thorburn painted him a picture of some bullfinches. The following year Jimmy guided Henry Emerson Tuttle, a professor at Groton College, Massachussetts famous for his bird etchings, on a short trip through the mountains. Tuttle was so enthusiastic that he wrote, "I never had four more enjoyable days in the open than those spent with you" and sent along a dry-point etching of a goshawk in appreciation.

Although Jimmy had at least a passing acquaintance with these interesting artists, his relationship with others went much deeper. Carl Rungius remained his favourite as well as his close personal friend and confidant, even though their relationship underwent some changes during the twenties. Jimmy could not afford to provide his horses and men at bargain rates indefinitely and since by the early twenties he had accumulated nine of Carl's paintings in return for doing so the two agreed that the artist should pay the going rate when Jimmy had an outfit available. If he did not, Carl would hire the services of one of the area's other outfitters. As a result, by the mid-twenties Carl had begun going out with Jim Boyce, who had often accompanied him when he worked for Jimmy before going into business for himself.

Similarly, during their early visits to Banff the Rungiuses had often stayed with the Simpsons, occupying the small saddle and tack shed adjacent to the house. But with the growing Simpson family, this was no longer feasible by the early twenties, and Jimmy therefore took matters into his own hands. A few years previously he had acquired two beautiful, large vacant lots on Cave Avenue, the road to the Cave and Basin, and in 1921 he suggested that Carl purchase them and build a studio home for summer and fall use to complement his winter studio in Manhattan. Rungius worried about the cost, but Jimmy convinced him that it would allow him more time in the mountains and the leisure to work up his paintings in the area that inspired them. He also promised that, if Carl agreed, he would personally handle the contracting for the building, to ensure that it met the artist's exact needs. Rungius eventually relented and purchased the lots. Over the winter of 1921-22 Jimmy had the home built, while responding almost daily to the concerns and changes that the artist wrote him about from New York. When it was completed, "The Paintbox," as Jimmy suggested it be named, became the headquarters for Carl's mountain activities for the next 30 years, allowing him to become a much more complete wilderness artist than otherwise would have been possible. Jimmy would always take great pride in having contributed towards this.

Another important American artist with whom Jimmy developed a close relationship in these years was Belmore Browne. A native of Staten Island, New York who had studied art at the New York School of Art and the Academie Julien in Paris, Browne was an extremely accomplished outdoorsman with a noteworthy reputation for Alaskan exploration. In 1901-02 he had served as artist and hunter on an American Museum of Natural History expedition from the Aleutians to the head of the Yukon River and in 1906, 1910 and 1912 was involved in mountaineering attempts on the continent's highest peak, Mount McKinley. On the 1912 trip he and fellow climber Herschel Parker succeeded in ascending to within 450 feet of the summit and were able to disprove the claim of one of the members of the 1906 expedition, Dr. Frederick Cook, that he had achieved the first ascent. On the same trip he shot what stood for 20 years as the world's record Alaskan brown bear. The story, published in his 1913 book *The Conquest of Mount McKinley*, gained Browne much notoriety and at the same time he began to be recognized for his artistic talents, particularly in the field of mountain landscapes.

Although Browne was a member of the Camp Fire Club of America after 1915, he had never met Jimmy before his first visit to Banff in 1921. He had probably heard of the delights of the Rockies for an outdoorsman and artist from Rungius, as they were fellow members of the Salmagundi Art Club as well as the Camp Fire Club. Jimmy later recalled his appearance in the Rockies: "Belmore Browne just showed up in Banff. I am sure he, like Carl, wanted new territory for his art ambitions. The first thing I knew we met and that was that for as long as he was west." An additional reason for his beginning to frequent Banff was undoubtedly related to the fact that by this time he had a wife and young children who could not easily travel to Alaska.

The Browne family took up residence for the summer of 1921 in a home on Spray Avenue and in the fall went on a pack trip to Shadow Lake. Browne was capable of taking care of the horses himself, but Jimmy provided him with a few head of stock and some good advice. This became the first of an annual summer visit to the Rockies for the Brownes, who lived in their combined home and studio in Banff, named Illahee Lodge, and went on frequent outings so Belmore could sketch and paint. In the fall of 1923 he was invited to accompany the hunting party of Philadelphia attorney Clement Wood, outfitted and guided by Jimmy, and by the mid-twenties the family's trips often took them to Bow Lake, where Jimmy provided for them at his camp. In her diary Mrs. Browne exclaimed, "A wonderful site Jim Simpson has here and I am completely carried away with the beauty of it all and what Jim has done here." She described the cabin as having "a fireplace and a sort of

assembly room hung with fine skins and a few photos but very comfortable." Her young daughter Evelyn was impressed by the long ride
around the shoreline in the water to Jimmy's camp, an experience
enjoyed by many early visitors:

*After the pause at the edge of the lake the leader waves and off we go on
the long and lovely trip around the lake to camp. The sloshing of the
horses feet through the water and the grinding of their hoofs on the gravel
underwater makes a considerable racket and it is hard to hear one
another over the din. George and I were ecstatic, we were usually
relegated to the end of our pack train and followed behind Jim's big pack
train and all his guests on horseback. So when George and I hit the lake
the whole pack train of some fifty horses were splashing their way ahead
of us around the curve of the lake. It was an unforgetable sight and sound
as the long pack train splashed the two miles through the water's edge
home to camp. . .*

*Then we came out on the flat, picked up a good trail, forded the creek
by camp up a little bank and into the rope corral Jim used for the horses.
And there was a red-headed Jim grinning and his crew of cowboys, the
big tent fly for meals and Tommy Frayne getting us hot biscuits and tea
over the long cooking fire and above on a little rise was the Octagonal
Cabin.*

Equally dramatic was the opportunity for those already in camp to
observe a pack train coming around the shore. Evelyn Browne described
it as looking like "a brightly colored bead necklace with all the different
colored horses and the colorful jackets of the riders fringed below with
a line of silver spray as the horses splashed the familiar way to camp and
freedom."

Jimmy's friendship with the Browne family would last the rest of his
life and on several occasions he would have the opportunity to watch
Belmore work on a painting, sometimes in the company of Rungius as
well. Over the years Jimmy would acquire several of his works, a
particular favourite being a view of the Bow Glacier as seen from his
camp, done shortly after a Browne family visit in 1928.

Although he had not thought much about the size and value of his art collection, by the mid-twenties Jimmy began to recognize that it was one of the finest in western Canada. So in 1928 when he heard that the Calgary Stampede was looking for good material to exhibit at an art salon to be held in conjunction with the exhibition and rodeo, he offered some of his paintings. E. T. Richardson, manager of the Stampede, to whom he wrote, turned the letter over to the selection committee and within a short time its head, Alexander Calhoun, was in touch with him to arrange to borrow 18 pieces. News of this reached the ears of Lars Haukaness, a Norwegian artist who had recently established an art school in conjunction with the Provincial Institute of Technology in Calgary. Haukaness had become friends with Jimmy when he was head of the art school in Winnipeg several years before; while visiting the mountains he had borrowed a tepee and horses from Jimmy to undertake painting expeditions. He asked that after the paintings had been exhibited at the Stampede they be lent to the Institute for an exhibition in their art museum. Jimmy agreed and in August, 1928 Calhoun wrote, "Your pictures were a big feature in our display at the Stampede and they have made a very fine display at the Museum." The popularity of the collection with the public would lead to several similar requests for loans in the years ahead and ultimately to its deposit in a major western museum.

The important role that art was playing in Jimmy's life by the twenties resulted in his decision to pursue his own talents in this field. Since he learned well by observation, watching great artists such as Rungius and Browne at work gained him a great deal of knowledge; he later equated it to watching someone build fireplaces until you were able to do it yourself, even though you could never quite duplicate the results. But he contended that he was largely self-taught as an artist, and stated that everywhere he went in such beautiful country there was a picture waiting to be painted. There was some truth in this, for after a few false starts in oils, the medium of most of his artistic acquaintances, he turned his attention entirely to watercolours. He preferred them because so many tints were available in watercolours as compared to oils, each one of which was present in nature around him. To achieve the range of colours he desired, he would keep up to three boxes of watercolours going at one time. Jimmy's first attempts were rather crude big game subjects, perhaps because he was trying to emulate Rungius, but as the twenties progressed he turned his attention entirely to landscapes and his skills improved. He gave most of these works away to friends or clients as a keepsake, as he didn't feel that they were up to a standard suitable for sale.

Another interesting facet of Jimmy's love of art was its role in the development of one of his most abiding hobbies — philately. He first became interested in stamps "because the British stamps were so beautifully printed they were like little pictures and their artistic beauty made them attractive." Beginning in 1928 he contacted a few dealers and began to pick up some British colonials, focussing on the British West Indies and British North America. He found the hobby fun and relaxing, and began to extend his collection to include the relatively new field of air mail stamps. The common items were easily obtained, but the rare ones were more difficult and on occasion cost him a good deal of money. Jimmy's response to a fellow collector when discussing this was that "the stamp hobby is expensive but so is the hobby of collecting money." Nonetheless, as one who always minded his pennies, when one of his treasures was lost his famous temper came to the fore. A classic case was reported by friend and fellow naturalist Dan McCowan in his book *Hilltop Tales*:

On the evening of a winter's day some years ago, I had occasion to visit Simpson in his home. Entering the house I was at once struck by the unusual silence brooding over the premises. Upon the walls of the living-room hung many fine paintings of mountain sheep, and goat, elk, moose and other mammals, all from the gifted brush of Carl Rungius. These creatures, at the moment, looked down upon a regular log-jam of upturned tables, chairs and other miscellaneous bits of household furni-ture. Scattered about was a litter of books, periodicals, ash-trays and gramophone records. In fact, the room bore some resemblance to a terminal moraine. . .

In addition to activities already mentioned Simpson at this time was keenly interested in philately. The day of my visit, which had dawned clear and sunny, he had received from a dealer in New York a postage stamp for which he had paid ten dollars. This stamp in some mysterious manner had disappeared, hence the topsy-turvey appearance and tense atmosphere of the living-quarters and the non-appearance of other members of the family. Some hours previously, in the gathering twilight of a domestic hurricane, the lady of the house had retired in dudgeon; the children likewise beat a hasty and tearful retreat, while on into the night did Father persist in hectic but fruitless search for the missing item...

It was clearly no time for pleasantry, or friendly fireside chat, so offering condolence and bidding him "Good night" I expressed the opinion that with the coming of the day the missing stamp would undoubtedly turn up. Sure enough it did. Next morning while dressing he found it, or rather its pale shadow, adhering firmly to the heel of his own shoe. It was so hopelessly downtrodden that of what had recently been a well-conditioned and valuable postage stamp only the watermark remained and even that was hopelessly scuffed.

Despite the odd such maddening occurrence, Jimmy persisted and as time went on he began to hone his collection specifically to Canadian imperfects and international airmails. That he made some excellent buys in these areas is attested to by his correspondence with numerous stamp dealers all over North America and Europe. For example, in November, 1930 G. P. Bainbridge, a Vancouver dealer, wrote: "You sure made a Real Buy on those imperfect mint blocks of Quebec issue. A set of pairs recently fetched £7-10-0 at London auction and they must be 10 times as scarce in blocks." Unfortunately, he was just hitting his collecting stride when the Depression set in and his activities had to be curtailed somewhat; he had to sell off of a good part of his colonial collection in order to be able to keep up with the imperfects and airmails at all.

One last important interest that Jimmy began to develop during the twenties was writing for outdoor periodicals. His earlier literary efforts, such as the piece about Rungius' goat hunt, had been done only for fun and were meant solely for the entertainment of his friends. But reading numerous stories on hunting and the outdoors in sporting magazines of the day, some by clients he had outfitted and guided, convinced him that he could write equally entertaining material. He began to keep school scribblers for jotting down stories when he had some free time or when an idea came to him that could be worked up into a more complete story later on.

His first success in writing came as somewhat of a surprise when in a fit of pique in 1923 he wrote a piece titled "The Tourist Sportsman," which laid out the things his clients were wont to do that caused him grief and anguish. It was created in response to the many articles written from the dudes' point of view, some of which made it sound like they did everything on the trip and the guide was merely along for the ride. Jimmy wrote about a variety of incidents that had driven him to distraction, such as when he had nearly been killed by a client and when another one had taken his newly sharpened axe and cut wood with a rock for a chopping block. He fired the piece off to Hy Watson, editor of *Field and Stream*, the official publication of the Campfire Club of America, and much to his amazement he received a letter indicating that they wanted to publish it and enclosing a cheque for $25. This initial success was followed by a series of columns written for the *Calgary Daily Herald*, which had begun to publish a weekly fish and game page in cooperation with the Alberta Fish and Game Association in 1928. Jimmy's great knowledge of wild game led to some interesting articles on their habits and behaviour, such as "Can Wild Animals Swim?" in which he discussed the subject from his years of observation in the wilderness. Again, while he wrote mostly for fun and relaxation, the income earned from these articles was welcome, and it would become increasingly important to him as the Depression began to tighten its grip on his business.

CHAPTER TEN
Num-Ti-Jah

As with businesses the world over, Jimmy's livelihood was to be inalterably affected by the Depression years of the thirties. Not only were there fewer clients for his outfitting operations, but the entire tourism industry underwent a fundamental change. Gone were the days when the horse was in the ascendancy in the Canadian Rockies, and replacing many of the major trails were roads built to handle the transportation mode of choice, automobiles and busses. It was a measure of Jimmy's foresight that he recognized the importance of these changes while they were occurring and was able to adapt to and even profit from them.

Actually, the early part of the Depression turned out to be rather good for his trail business. He had several important parties reserved for 1929 and when the market crashed in October he was out hunting with one of the best of them, John K. Howard and Samuel Peabody, Philadelphia financiers who had booked him at $1,500 for an entire month. They had arrived in a new Ford car after driving from Reno, Nevada over the "Grand Canyon Route," one of several new roads that linked Banff with major centres in the United States. Their decision to drive resulted in an immediate and unexpected benefit for Jimmy when Howard and Peabody learned of the crash after coming in off the trail:

We left Lake Louise and went up the Pipestone River and all the way they were telling one another as they were riding together how many millions they were going to make while they were out on this month's hunting trip. When we got back they put on a horrible banquet for us, of course, but when they saw the New York newspapers they said, "We've got to get back and we don't have time to drive." So they gave me the car and said, "If we ever come back we'll pick it up again." Howard didn't come back for fifteen or twenty years and when he did he asked, "Where's the old car?" I said, "Oh, I wrapped it around three or four trees and backed it into a creek with three kids in it. But it was a damn good car — the last time I saw it, it was carrying some people up to Lake Louise.

That Jimmy should have had some difficulty driving this gift horse was not surprising because he had never owned a car and had never learned to drive, preferring as he did, a horse of a different sort. When he got up the nerve to try it, he caused some consternation on the streets of the town:

When I learned to drive I went down one of the side streets and then I went down the main street in our village of Banff. There wasn't many people on it and I thought, "Well, I'll go down right to the end of it and turn around where there is hardly anybody." But when I got about half way down there seemed to be nobody around and I twisted over the wheel very quickly, spun round, missed a silent policeman by an inch, missed a live one by half-an-inch, and when the two other wheels came down on the ground I drove away and they never even stopped me. They were too surprised.

Jimmy jr. later attested to the fact that Jimmy never really understood anything mechanical and especially not this car. One day when he was still a young boy his father wheeled the car into a gas station. "Jim," he said, "I think we better fill 'er up with gas." "And check the oil," chimed in the youngster. Jimmy stared at him incredulously and blurted out, "What in the hell do you mean, does it burn oil too?"

The good fortune continued for a bit longer. His bookings were so heavy for 1930 that he had to turn down some of his favourite old customers, including Alfred Castle and members of the Vaux family. In the fall he took out a hunting party sent to him by Jim Wilson which included the son of his friend P. H. Batten, president of the Twin Disc Manufacturing Co. of Racine, Wisconsin. John Batten, a lad of only 18 and a student at Andover Academy at the time, would go on to become one of America's foremost big game hunters and would be a client and friend of Jimmy's for many years thereafter. According to Jimmy's later account, things got even better after that:

I was tremendously lucky. I got a telegram from a man in Philadelphia who wanted to bring out his entire family. He was a maker of car bodies for Fisher. He wanted to bring all the family and two maids and two or three visitors to stay at Bow Lake for July and August and then he wanted me to take the entire family on a month's big game hunt. I sent a telegram back saying it would cost $15,000 and he wired back saying "make it 10 and I'll come." I made a record trip to the telegraph office and wired "you're on." ... While they were here I had them out climbing and I had to send out some of my best men with them. I took them out for two months and had about 35 head of horses for the hunting trip. That summer, which was the worst of the Depression, I took in about $18,000 and all of the fellows got to work.

While the figure was probably exaggerated, the story illustrates that it was not until well into the Depression that Jimmy began to feel its effects, but then he had to be resourceful to survive. Jimmy was never one to have any spare cash for such eventualities, and much of the profits of the twenties had gone into his stamp collection and even moreso into the stock market. A great believer in the value of the country's natural resources, he had begun buying a good deal of mining stock in the late twenties, and despite the warnings of friends like Billy Beach who were in the know, he continued to buy even after the crash. Ultimately, most of these investments became virtually worthless.

By 1931 many of Jimmy's old clients were choosing to take shorter, less expensive trips. He began to offer his summer guests more frequent and cheaper camping trips, usually based out of Bow Lake, as opposed to the more costly moving pack trips. That fall he had several costly cancellations, but he was able to report to one of his clients that he had "a good season in spite of the conditions." Soon afterwards, however, his regular customers, feeling the pinch of the times and not wishing to abandon their accustomed outings in the Rockies, began to request lower rates. For example, Henry S. Kingman of Minneapolis, whom Jimmy had met when he was out as one of the first American skiers in the Rockies in 1930, wrote in June, 1933: "I would like to take a short trip with Thorington to Peyto Lake. It was my thought that with your facilities at Hector Lake, that possibly you could afford to give us an extra low price on this trip. Times are considerably different than they used to be for most of us, and we can only take these trips today at a minimum of expense." In subsequent correspondence he requested two pack horses and a man to cook at Peyto Lake for $300 and when Jimmy replied that this was impossible Kingman wrote, "Give us the best you can for $300, we'll have to take less for that price." Similarly, when Kingman and Thorington decided to take a longer, three week trip the following summer, Kingman indicated that they would make their own way to Bow Lake and that they then wanted Jimmy to outfit them from there to the Freshfields and return "for not more than $550." As his rates for a similar trip before the Depression would have been $1,000, Jimmy's reply was to the point:

I don't think I want to take you for the price you state. Unfortunately I have to keep a family eating and to take you for the price of $550.00 is to pay the expenses with a very minimum of compensation for the use of the outfit and equipment which after all is my stock in trade.

You paid $300 for ten days last year and admitted it was reasonable. I supplied two men. This season you want 21 days and I have to supply three, and the only way it can be done and let you go at all reasonable is to go myself and save the paying of the extra wage. That means I have to outfit for 6 people. . .

I doubt if any outfitter would do it for the price you state. The Brewster people charge my prices and they, their outfitting end, made an assignment last winter and are paying 25 cents on the dollar but they tried to make liquor and business combine.

The very least I will even consider is $600. and of that $200 on acceptance to pay the provision account and the incidentals, not wages, before leaving. Otherwise it would pay me better to fool around with fishing parties to Hector, Pipestone and Bow Lake. I would make more money and less expense. There is reason in all things H.S. but I am not so stuck on camping that I want to put in time at it after the novelty has been missing many, many years.

Kingman got the point and agreed to the terms that Jimmy stated.

As the income from his tourist outfitting operations began to plummet with the deepening of the Depression, Jimmy began to examine other ways to supplement it. At one point he looked into becoming a part-time life insurance salesman for London Life, but they were interested only in full-time agents. He did make an agreement with the Calgary Power Company to do periodic readings of a water guage they had installed in Hector Lake, with each reported reading being worth $1.00. But it was to be the Banff-Jasper Highway project that would provide the best temporary source of income — a project that would also help to secure his future livelihood.

As mentioned, Jimmy had always been a great promotor of the area north of Lake Louise, but for many years his arguments had fallen on deaf ears. The CPR had been more interested in developing tourism facilities in conjunction with their main line, and they left the more remote areas to smaller interests. When it had first become involved in building roads to the park in the twenties, the Dominion Government had concentrated on connecting Banff with United States destinations to the south by means of the Banff-Windermere Highway and the upgrading of the road to Calgary. It was not until 1929 that the Dominion and British Columbia governments agreed to jointly construct the Big Bend Highway around the northern arc of the Columbia River, linking existing roads at Revelstoke and Golden and providing a direct route from the prairies through the parks to the Pacific coast. Both federal and provincial contributions to this project had been cut drastically at the beginning of the Depression and it was only saved from total failure by the passing of the Unemployment and Farm Relief Act of 1931, which provided the funding and men on relief that would allow the work to proceed. The same act allowed work to begin on the Banff-Jasper Highway, another labour-intensive project that would allow the government to put men to work building a road to connect the two major mountain tourism centres on the Canadian Pacific and Canadian National Railways, Banff and Jasper.

According to Jimmy, he and a number of other Banff residents were instrumental in convincing the government to undertake the Banff-Jasper Highway project, recalling that "we got in touch with Bennett and asked him if he could get a road open from here through to Jasper." Whether they were influential in the decision or not, it would certainly benefit all of them. When work got underway north of Lake Louise in the fall of 1931, Jimmy was able to secure one of the first contracts for blazing a trail from Lake Louise to Bow Lake:

I blazed the high trail. Bill McCardell, of Bankhead, got the contract to get some men and have it cut. Howard Sibbald was the chief game warden at the time and he got me to come up and blaze the trail. He says, "How much will you charge?" I said, "Seventy-five dollars." He said, "It's a good price, there's lots of blazing to do." So they gave me the contract and I came up and did it all in one day. I came up in the evening and got as far as Hector Lake, camped under a tree all night, finished it the next day and went back to Lake Louise and caught the train to Banff. Sibbald said, "You've done it in that time, that's making a lot of money." I said, "Yes, and doing a lot of work too."

This reconnaissance work was followed by a location survey done by an engineer and a survey party. These parties required a pack train for travel and the delivery of weekly supplies and, as Jimmy's horses were the closest at hand, he was the one most often called upon to supply horses and equipment. For each pack horse he supplied to the survey he received fifty cents per day, and sometimes he provided his personal services as well. Because of his great knowledge of the country the road was traversing, he was also periodically asked by the road builders to give advice on routes, the location of culverts and other matters. He found this very frustrating, as "in the government service you can't give them advice, they're supposed to take it from Ottawa and they don't know as much as those in Banff." In his many dealings with the government over the years, Jimmy would often express these feelings.

Construction of the highway proceeded slowly because of the requirement that as much of it be done by human labour as possible, in keeping with the relief orientation of the project. The work consisted of the clearing and stumping of a right-of-way between 50 and 60 feet wide, the filling of low areas and placing of culverts for drainage, grading using two-horse fresnoes, and finally gravel surfacing. The section alongside Bow Lake caused the road builders as much trouble as it had always caused Jimmy with his pack train because of its wetness and the muskegy consistency of the shoreline. It took the dedication of some 25 teams with wheelers hauling fill the better part of a season to solve the problem. Construction to the summit of Bow Pass was therefore not completed until the fall of 1935. Highway engineer Ted Garrett recalled Jimmy's first drive along the section beside Bow Lake, when his car threw a wheel. He fumed, "If that was a horse with a broken leg I would know what to do — I would shoot it, but what in hell do you do with this thing?"

During the period of construction, several of Jimmy's clients wrote to him to express their feelings about the new road. Dr. Thorington offered:

It seems a bit sad to me that the road is going up into the country where we had so much fun. It was about the last stand of the pack-train, and it is a shame to trade that experience for the sake of the few cars that will rush through. Someday when you are running a garage and tea-room at Bow Lake, and want to see how cayuses look, just run down here and I'll show you some movies of the good old days.

Jim Wilson felt the same way and wrote, "I presume this will be a good thing for you and a lot of people, but I know from one angle you agree with me in rather hating to see the thing go through." Jimmy understood their feelings and even agreed with them to a point, but he was realistic enough to know that it was the future that was of the most importance:

I feel like you as regards the motor road up into the north country. When I recall the old days when I used to snowshoe and sleep out at night under the stars & a spruce with 20 below as the only covering it makes me feel that I don't want to see the same landmarks from an auto. I suppose the wind will blow with the same frigidity: the same ridges will be wind-swept & the same hollows will be drifted full even though the motor road passes over or by them, but to me the landscape will hold a blight or a scar that will never heal. Oh well, times must and will change. The young-sters of the present day accept the changed conditions as a matter of course just as we did in our day & I suppose we ought to look ahead instead of backward. After all the trail in the making is more interesting than the one made previously, like the peak to be climbed for the first time instead of the last.

Given such sentiments, it was not surprising that he was equally happy to agree with Alfred Castle, who predicted that the road was "going to make your camps very accessible and, I hope, profitable some day."

It is not entirely clear whether Jimmy had forseen the importance of the future development of Bow Lake when he requested a lease from Harkin; sometimes he claimed he had, other times he said it was just good luck to be in the right place when the opportunity came along. In any event, with the beginning of construction on the road it became apparent that he was going to be well situated to handle some of the needs of travellers along the new route. During the early thirties, though, he was in no position to take advantage of the situation, as he had no cash available for development. That problem was only to be solved later in the decade when the exploits of his two daughters provided funds for the family enterprise.

Despite the fact that their father made his living from horses and the wilderness, Margaret and Mary had been brought up as proper young ladies. Jimmy's opinions on raising girls were quite Victorian, although once in a while he did allow them to ride the horses. Mary Simpson recalled her first ride on one of her father's old stalwarts, Prince Joseph. As soon as she got in the saddle he bucked her off and, looking up from the shrubbery, she heard her father laugh and say, "You could have tied your shoes while you were up in the air." But while they might get the odd ride when he was not busy, the girls were not allowed to help out or to be about when he was doing business. Instead they attended to their school work and spent most of their time under their mother's watchful eye. Her love of figure skating set the tone of their upbringing and, as mentioned, for as long as they could remember they were on skates. This Jimmy viewed with a somewhat jaundiced eye, and he was heard to crack on occasion that he would have to build a skating rink on the kitchen floor so things wouldn't slow down too much around the house. However, his view would change as the girls gained success, and eventually he would become extremely proud of their accomplishments.

In 1928, at the ages of eleven and nine respectively, Margaret and Mary made their debut as the Simpson Sisters in the Banff Winter Carnival and were an instant local hit. At the same time they came to the attention of a visiting Saskatoon skating professional, Gordon Thompson, who was doing some teaching in Calgary at the time. Thompson gave the girls some instruction and was so impressed with their talents that following the 1929 Winter Carnival he contacted Jimmy and asked if the girls might be allowed to participate with him in the carnival at Saskatoon. Jimmy agreed, and the Simpson Sisters were launched on their skating career. They appeared with Thompson at several shows in Saskatchewan and went on a number of short tours to the west coast, skating for the Rotary Club shows in Vancouver and the Shrine Club shows in Seattle and Portland.

Living in Banff, it was hard for Margaret and Mary to get the professional tutelage they needed once they had progressed beyond the level of the instructors in the area. That, and the rather snobbish attitude of most figure skating clubs, made it difficult for the girls to progress after their early triumphs. In 1934 Jimmy took matters in hand and wrote to an acquaintance, Harry Sifton of Toronto, a member of an influential political family, to ask for information on skating in that city. Sifton provided the contacts that allowed the girls to go to Toronto for instruction that year. The Simpson Sisters' first major appearance occurred in April when the Figure Skating Club of Minneapolis and the Norwegian American Athletic Club jointly organized a skating program featuring Sonja Henie, the reigning Olympic and World's Champion woman figure skater. The Simpson Sisters performed a duet, and each of them also performed solo in the program.

One of the people who witnessed their performance in Minneapolis was Donald Bain, a leading Winnipeg sportsman and figure skater, and the next winter he made arrangements for Mary and Margaret to receive instruction at the Winnipeg Winter Club, while staying at his own home. Mary in particular progressed very rapidly and in 1936, at the age of 18, she competed in the Canadian Figure Skating Championships in Montreal, placing fourth. Meanwhile, the increasing popularity of figure skating at this time led to the beginning of a new phenomenon in skating circles, the touring ice revue. Sonja Henie's manager approached

Jimmy about handling the girls, but he felt that if they were going to make it they should do it on their own. For 1935 and 1936 the girls continued to skate as amateurs, spending part of each year on an ice show circuit that performed in the north-eastern United States featuring such American skating stars as Evelyn Chandler and Shipstad & Johnson.

In 1937 they turned professional when Billie negotiated a contract with a new international ice revue known as "Gay Blades" which toured throughout the eastern United States over the winter of 1937-38. While the show featured Olympic champion Karl Schaefer and Mirabel Vinson, the largest round of applause was often saved for the "Sweethearts of the Canadian Rockies." Drawing on their Canadian background, Billie and Margaret planned a "Mountie" number using costumes that looked like the uniform of the country's famous police force.

Until they went on tour with "Gay Blades," Billie had always accompanied the girls during their performances. However, with the heavy travel schedule of the ice revue and the fact that the girls were old enough to look after themselves, this was neither possible nor necessary. Consequently, neither Billie nor Jimmy were present for their triumphal tour. But because of Jimmy's wide circle of clientele, who lived in virtually every city in which the girls performed, they were kept informed of the Simpson Sisters' progress by letters from friends. For example, CPR architect Walter Painter and his wife Stella, close friends of the Simpsons, saw the girls debut in New York and immediately wrote with glowing reports: "The girls had them on their feet hollering for more last night. They were the idols of the Gardens. Billie deserves all the credit in the world for putting them over." Another friend, Myron Glasberg of St. Louis wrote, "Saturday night the 'Mountie' act literally stopped the show, and when after three or four curtain calls the announcer started on the next number the crowd drowned him out and insisted on an encore from the girls." These personal reports were soon backed up by newspaper clippings the Simpsons received as the tour progressed. The *New Haven Register* reported that "records fail to reveal these Canadian girls as dangerous contenders in figure skating competition, but for spectacular skating they are tops," while closer to home the *Calgary Albertan* reported on a Canadian Press byline that "Banff Girls Steal Show At New York."

The *New York Herald* carried a rather interesting report:

The two girls from Banff, the Misses Margaret and Mary Simpson, display unusual speed and stamina in their acrobatic pair and the energy comes from the strength gained in mountain climbing. The father of the sisters is one of Canada's foremost mountaineers and during the summer months the two girls are companions on the perilous climbs in the Canadian Rockies. The climbers take their skates along and when they find a glacier which is reasonably smooth they do their summer skating high above the timber line.

While obviously a bit of hyperbole engaged in by a zealous press agent for the show, the story was not as far fetched as it may have seemed. Jimmy, seeing an opportunity for the girls to practice during the summertime, used the Bow Glacier as a natural ice surface:

I made a rink up on the glacier for the girls after they turned professional. Mary and Margaret and I went up there first and Mary slipped on the ice because it was all pitted and said, "That's pretty hard to fall on." So I got an ice scrapper from Allan Mather and I went up there with it and a shovel and some sacking to cover the ice from the sun and made a skating rink on the first bench, smoothed it all off and then threw the tools down a crevasse. They had the time of their lives there. They used to walk right up the glacier, put on their skates and then skate. I thought if they were going to turn professional they might as well have something new.

Margaret and Mary's contract with "Gay Blades" earned between $350 and $450 per week, an amount Jimmy described as "real money at that time" considering their ages. The girls happily agreed to put the money to good use in improving the family fortunes, thereby giving Jimmy the wherewithal to expand his operation at Bow Lake during a period when building funds would otherwise have been almost impossible to come by.

In 1920, when he was doing the original development at Bow Lake, Jimmy had submitted a plan for a lodge building that was somewhat larger than the original octagonal cabin actually built. As work proceeded on the site, his conception of what was needed began to change, and in August, 1924 he informed the Parks Branch that he was preparing plans for a ten-room lodge. These plans were never submitted but he continued to think in terms of a larger lodge throughout the period from the issue of his lease in 1925 up until he actually began work on it in the summer of 1937. Hired to head the building operation was Vern Castella, who had proven his skills during the original construction at Bow Lake, and he was assisted by Karl Hansen, a fine Norwegian finishing carpenter from Calgary. Jimmy, Castella and Hansen worked out a plan as they went along, evolving a structure approximately 37 feet by 50 feet made of log and built on a stone base.

The structure required longer logs than those available at the altitude of Bow Lake and, fortunately, a ready supply was found at Silverhorn Creek, some ten miles north near Mistaya Lake, where a forest fire had swept through the timber in 1936. Two of Jimmy's men, Jack Harris and Louis Rae, spent much of the summer of 1937 cutting and skidding out the timber and then hauling it to Bow Lake over the recently completed stretch of the Banff-Jasper Highway. The road not only allowed for suitable building logs to reach the lake, it also provided some of the actual construction material for the lodge. During construction of the road, piles of rock from clearing the right-of-way had been made at intervals alongside it and these were eventually dynamited. The remains provided a ready source of stone for use in the foundation of Jimmy's lodge, and Jimmy jr. spent many days driving up and down the highway loading up a truck with the best pieces.

The off-the-cuff design for the lodge worked out reasonably well, but it was not perfect. As work progressed, Jimmy jr. asked his father about the shape of the roof and what would happen with the accumulation of snow. Jimmy impatiently dismissed the question, stating that it would slide off by itself. Actually, he didn't know how the roof was going to be designed, but he hoped that Castella would come up with something when the time arrived. His only requirement was that it be designed so that the winds sweeping down off the glacier would take the snow off the roof, since he would not always be present to clear it off in the winter. Ultimately Castella's solution to putting a roof on a building of such unusual shape required the construction of thirteen valleys, and Jimmy jr.'s doubts often came back to haunt him as he found himself up on top of the lodge shovelling off huge amounts of snow.

Despite such occasional problems with the lodge's design, Jimmy always defended its idiosyncracies. When he and architect Walter Painter were measuring off the windows and Painter noted that they weren't of uniform size, Jimmy said, "No, no any damn fool can do them to the same measure." "It takes a smart man to do it different and still make it look fine."

When work had progressed far enough to permit it, Jimmy began building the two fireplaces that were to provide the main sources of heat, one of them which was to be 25 feet high. He had never built a fireplace before but he had watched the mason who had built the one in his house closely and learned from observation. When later asked about this skill he stated,"I don't know, it's just one of those inexplicable things — it's a gift for everything I do." Substantial footings were needed to support the weight of these massive structures, requiring the digging of deep pits which were then filled with large boulders. Even the children were pressed into action to roll enough large rocks to fill the cavities. When the footings were complete and the work on the fireplace itself started, Jimmy used the best and most colourful remnants of the highway construction stone, which he had carefully put aside for this use. When the work was completed, a visitor expressed some doubt as to whether or not the larger fireplace would draw and Jimmy quipped, "Ha, it could draw the socks off your feet."

In typical Simpson fashion, Jimmy had gone ahead with the construction without informing the government of his plans or bothering to apply for a building permit. This came to the attention of Park Superintendent P. J. Jennings in September, 1938 and he called Jimmy into his office for an explanation. Jimmy said that he was proceeding with the work originally approved by Harkin, but substituting stone for some of the logs. When asked to submit architectural plans, Jimmy maintained that Painter had been working on them but that he had become ill and had been confined to the hospital, etc., etc., which prevented completion of the plans. Actually, Painter was busy on CPR work at the time and Jimmy could not get his attention for long enough to get him to come up to Bow Lake to prepare proper drawings.

In desperation, Jimmy made a suggestion to Superintendent Jennings: "Just to conform to the regulations as required would you send me up one of your staff architects at my expense sometime next week and let him make plans for what is now constructed under my informational direction. I will supply him with his noonday oats and undoubtedly he would like to be away from you all for a day." Jennings was not amused, and Jimmy had to continue to search for another solution. Ultimately he learned that Karl Hansen, the carpenter working with Castella on the building, had some skills in architectural design and he was given the job of drawing up what had essentially already been built. At the end of September, Jimmy wrote Jennings: "My architect, Mr. Carl Hansen of Calgary, who is at present on location will prepare a complete set of plans with out buildings such as electric light building or power house, and will add the present construction to the plans so that the Department can see what is proposed and also being done. The present building is really the original plans tremendously elaborated to conform with the site." Hansen's drawing was completed and submitted in November, 1938, and the building permit was issued in December. In the meantime Jimmy had applied for a permit to operate a seasonal hotel at Bow Lake, indicating that he had already spent $8,000 on the project and intended to spend $15,000 more before completing it in 1940.

Jimmy would continue to feud with Jennings about the development at Bow Lake and tax arrears on his various properties for several years. Eventually Jennings would be moved to complain to F. H. Williamson, Controller of the National Parks Bureau, that "unfortunately our efforts in many instances have been misconstrued by Mr. Simpson and he has on numerous occasions dealt directly with your office and also with members of the political parties in regard to certain of the subjects that have become contentious." Williamson commiserated with him but, knowing Jimmy, counselled patience:

It is clear that Mr. Simpson is labouring under a certain amount of economic pressure which, coupled with an obvious irascibility of temperament, has made him impatient of departmental procedure. Judging from experience in dealing with Mr. Simpson, threatened cancellation proceedings in the past have not been productive of satisfactory results. It is unquestionably a fact that he has, on the whole, contributed consider-able sums to the Exchequer and if given reasonable latitude it is felt that ultimately the arrears that have been permitted to accumulate will be paid off in full.

In September, 1940 Williamson made a personal appeal to Jimmy to heal the rift between he and Jennings, and thereafter matters cooled off considerably.

Even as work was proceeding on the lodge, the Simpsons were able to operate Bow Lake camp on a seasonal basis as early as 1937, with access on the highway available from Lake Louise. In fact, while the highway was being pushed up the valley towards the lake some enthu-siasts had driven as far as they could and had then hiked the rest of the way. Beginning in 1934, Billie cooked for guests in a tent near the Ram Pasture and she continued to do so with the assistance of Margaret and Mary when they were home from their skating exploits, while Jimmy jr. helped his father take care of the guests' other needs.

In naming the lodge, Jimmy had chosen the Stoney word "num-ti-gah" (later spelled "num-ti-jah") for the pine marten that had been so prevalent in the area during his trapping days, and in his advertising he referred to "Simpson's Num-Ti-Gah Lodge, Bow Lake" offering "rid-ing, fishing, boating, hiking, log cabin accommodation, lunches, tea, dinner." He continued to run his smaller operation at Hector Lake, comprised of two cabins and a boathouse, in conjunction with it, although his rights to this location were also a sore spot with the government. A number of his old customers took advantage of the opportunity to have spouses and friends stay at Bow Lake while they outfitted for a trip with him. Dr. Thorington booked a trip to the Thompson Pass area and the Freshfields with his friends Dr. Ladd, Eaton Cromwell and Georgia Engelhard for July, 1937 and made arrangements for his wife and two of her friends to stay at the lodge part of the time he was on the trail.

An increasing number of parties began making use of the facilities as the lodge took shape over the succeeding summers of 1938 and 1939. By the time the Banff-Jasper Highway officially opened in the summer of 1940, the building program was basically complete for the time being, and Num-Ti-Gah Lodge was one of only two accommodation and dining locations in the highway's 143 mile length between Lake Louise and Jasper. Its design featured a large central dining room of essentially rectangular shape with a smaller rectangular kitchen on one side and a similarly sized living room on the other, with the dining room and living room each boasting one of the beautiful fireplaces Jimmy had built. Upstairs there were six guest rooms and two bathrooms capable of accommodating twelve people, in addition to those staying in the cabins. The interior featured wood panelling to cover the stonework and natural log from that point upward, and the walls were decorated with Jimmy's art collection. One visitor remarked that in appearance and atmosphere it reminded her more of a home than a lodge.

Jimmy's original idea that "sometime I'll build a shack here," which had come to mind some forty-odd years before when he had first seen the magnificent campsite from the back of his horse, had been realized in a way that he had never dreamed of.

CHAPTER ELEVEN

Passing the Torch

As Jimmy wrote Henry Kingman in 1933, "I am not so stuck on camping that I want to put in time at it after the novelty has been missing many, many years." This statement pretty well summed up his feelings after 40 years of outfitting and guiding — it was a business that provided a living, but most of what was unique or exciting about it had long since disappeared. On top of this, his pack train was now getting pretty long in the tooth and would have to be rejuvenated if he were going to continue, a considerable expense at a time when he was attempting to muster all the funds he could for the development of the lodge. In the midst of this, nature intervened and settled the matter. After wintering his horses on the Red Deer River during the winter of 1936-37, he reported to the government "eighty percent of my packtrain died through deep snow conditions and advanced age."

While his own age and inclinations no longer made the outfitting business attractive, he realized that it could still be a viable part of the operations at Bow Lake. There were still people who wished to go on pleasure pack trips; there were still a reasonable number of sportsmen interested in hunting in the Rockies who would find the lodge an attractive headquarters; and there was a definite need to make a day trip pony business one of the attractions if Num-Ti-Gah were going to become popular with tourists. The answer to these needs lay in his son and heir Jimmy jr., who had been brought up with all the skills and horse sense that Jimmy could impart. Although he was only a lad of 14 when the winter snows decimated his father's herd, he, like his sisters, wanted to contribute whenever and wherever he could. As Jimmy related to the government in 1940, when someone complained he was working without a guides' license, this meant that his son took over the ownership and operation of the outfitting business:

All stock is owned by my son; bought and paid for with his own funds through the agency of his sisters. Jim Simpson jr. has paid his dues to your Department ever since he owned his own packstring. He is the licensed guide not I. He has his own Brand and Bills of Sale and had he been old enough at the time Magistrate Hunter would have put through the necessary papers relative to the sale of all equipment & saddlery etc.

Jimmy jr. had learned the business of packing, camping and hunting the hard way, as a young man helping his father keep the larder full during the rough times of the Depression years. With little cash and few parties to outfit, it came to be Jimmy's habit to go on a hunt in the late fall and to bring in as much meat as his horses could carry, in order to feed his family over the winter. Although only in his early teens, young Jimmy accompanied him and quickly learned how to live off the land. In 1937 Jimmy jr. and his father were caught in a blizzard in the Harrison Flats area and Jimmy jr. was called upon to round up the horses, which necessitated wading an ice-choked stream with bare feet. Then they had to break trail and they underwent severe hardships in getting the pack string back to Lake Louise. Once they had arrived and unloaded the meat, Jimmy instructed his son to take the horses back to the Red Deer, where they would winter, and then to hike out to meet him at the Little Pipestone Warden Cabin. Young Jimmy did as he was told, driving the horses by himself back over the trail they had just traversed, leaving them on the Red Deer and then hiking for several days to make the rendezvous. When he arrived he was so tired that he couldn't even eat the food that his father had prepared for him. Although such occurrences made Jimmy seem a hard taskmaster to his son, it was the same type of toughening up Jimmy had undergone to prepare himself for a life in the wilderness 40 years before.

Actually, the transition of responsibility for the outfitting operations did not happen overnight; rather, it was something that evolved as he gained years and experience. In 1937 Jimmy took out Lillian Gest, one of Caroline Hinman's former girls, and noted mountaineer Katie Gardiner for some climbing in the Mount Bryce region. Jimmy acted as guide and young Jimmy went as a packer along with Louis Rae and Jack Harris. The following autumn, 1938, they took out a party headed by Norman Lougheed of Calgary to the Clearwater River area for hunting, and on the certificate registering the party Jimmy jr.'s name was listed as guide while Jimmy's appeared under the category of "camp helper." That same fall Jimmy jr. guided his first party without Jimmy's help — Jack Batten and his bride on a honeymoon trip to Fish Lakes. After the hunting season ended, he went off to Technical School in Calgary to learn automotive mechanics, and graduated in 1939. The following two winters saw him sharpening his considerable hockey skills, playing junior first for the Edmonton Athletics and then for the Winnipeg Monarchs, and returning to Bow Lake in the summer to run the outfit.

His gradual withdrawal from active guiding and outfitting and concomitant concentration on the building and operating of the lodge meant a major change in lifestyle for Jimmy. Billie and the children now worked at his side and the trials and tribulations of the trail were replaced by those associated with dealing with the lodge and the guests on a day-to-day basis. Just how hectic this could make life was witnessed by family friend Catharine Whyte while she was at Bow Lake on a painting trip in July, 1940. A group of seven boys and girls from Georgia stopped at the lodge for lunch and wanted to visit the Bow Glacier, so some walked around the lakeshore and others went across in a boat. When a storm blew up Jimmy became worried that all seven would try get back quickly in the boat and he hurriedly rowed across the lake to make sure that they wouldn't, waiting an hour for them in the pouring rain:

They had had a wonderful time & felt real snow etc. & were pretty damp as well, for there was a good shower with the rain. They all had tea & lots of people began arriving for the night until they were full up in no time. There were all sorts of license plates outside, N.Y., Penna., Minnesota, Washington, California, Manitoba and one other. Mrs. Walker from Banff came with her husband & friends and there was much going on. Another storm came up very quickly to drench the fishermen standing on the shore, and with it a terrific wind. The lake had been so calm before but the wind in no time whipped up the waves & really it was a pretty bad storm. Suddenly a lady who had come with her family rushed downstairs & there was much excitement. Her two small daughters aged 15 and nine were out in the boat and way on the other side of the lake. Luckily they had the best boat and somehow the oldest girl kept her head & kept rowing a little, just enough to keep it from tipping over. The wind blew them right across to this side of the lake. Jim and the father jumped in the other boat & tried to get out to them but didn't make much headway. They were bobbing about, the rain lashing down & the wind roaring. Evidently the two children quite enjoyed the experience & the little one wasn't scared at all; they certainly were plucky but everyone else had a good scare.

That was almost enough for one day and after some 20 people had had dinner we began wondering when the Phillips family would get back from a climbing trip they had gone on. They had taken their lunch and started after breakfast and at supper time they weren't back. Jim again rowed across the lake & met Mrs. Phillips and one daughter. . .

Despite the fact that many such busy days followed the opening of the Banff-Jasper Highway in 1940, the immediate future held some severe setbacks for the lodge and, indeed, for the Simpson family itself. The hardest blow came in 1941 when Jimmy and Billie lost their eldest daughter, Margaret.

After their successful season with the "Gay Blades" ice revue in 1937-38, the company dissolved and Margaret's and Mary's contract was picked up by the booking agents M.C.A. Thereafter they appeared at several locations, including the International Casino in Times Square over the the summer, with the "Ice Follies" revue for several shows, and on a tour of the eastern United States. In the fall of 1938 Vincent Astor of New York approached M.C.A. to engage the services of several of the skaters they had under contract, in order to begin a new concept he had in mind. This involved offering New Yorkers the opportunity to experience an evening at the posh St. Regis Hotel that would include dinner and dancing as well as skating entertainment featuring some of the foremost stars of the day. The "Iridium Room" held its gala opening in October, 1938 with the Simpson Sisters headlining alongside Nathan Wally, Dorothy Lewis and Sam Jarvis. The idea proved to be a popular one, and the girls performed there until Mary became sick in the spring of 1939 and was ordered by her doctor to take a year off skating. Margaret found employment as a figure skating teacher in Boston, working for Walter Brown, general manager of Garden Arena Corporation, and while doing so met and fell in love with his handsome young sportsman brother, Paul Vincent Brown. In June, 1940 they were married and they seemed poised to live a happy life together in which skating would undoubtedly have played a major role, when tragedy struck. In the summer of 1941 the couple visited Jimmy and Billie at Bow Lake, helped out with the business, and were returning to the east in September through Wyoming when Margaret became ill. A week later she died of a ruptured tubal pregnancy with her husband, mother and sister at her side.

The loss of their daughter at the young age of 24 with such a bright future ahead of her affected Jimmy and Billie deeply. Although he was accustomed to the life and death rhythm that had always been part of existence in the mountains, Jimmy found Margaret's death by what was then a little understood medical condition hard to accept. He wrote to the doctor who had cared for her in an attempt to gain some understanding, and after they received the explanation he and Billie rarely mentioned Margaret in public again — it was just too painful for them. Her partner now gone, Mary returned to the east and became involved in teaching figure skating, worked for a period on the production of "Ice Capades," and eventually began a ten-year career as a skating professional in Omaha, Nebraska. During the short break from her skating work in the summer, she would return to Bow Lake to help out where she could.

The family's personal pain was made all the harder to cope with because of the deepening effects of the war. North American tourism remained at a high level through 1941; Europe was closed to travel, and many armed service personnel in training also visited Bow Lake during furlough. However, 1942 was a completely different matter because of the government's decision in late 1941 to impose rationing to conserve supplies of rubber and gasoline for military purposes. In March, 1942 all sightseeing trips by bus or car were prohibited, and the flow of visitors slowed to a trickle. Not only were few guests able to reach Bow Lake, but Jimmy himself had difficulty in getting the tires and gasoline he needed to keep the lodge supplied.

In the midst of this situation, Jimmy was involved in trying to renew his original lease at Bow Lake, which was due to expire on August 31, 1942. His first correspondence with the Banff Park Superintendent on the matter in 1941 had indicated that he wished the lease to be renewed in the name of his two daughters, apparently in recognition of the contribution they had made. However, when writing further about the matter at the beginning of 1942, Jimmy noted that "events of the past year have made that impossible" and asked that it be renewed in his name instead. At the same time, he asked that the original four acres be extended to ten acres so that it would encompass his corrals and his source of water, both of which were currently outside the lease. The Parks Branch was generally in favour of renewing his rights at Bow Lake, but they wanted a dispute over his development at Hector Lake settled and they wanted to be clear about the type of rights to be granted in the renewal. The Hector Lake matter went back to 1927, when Jimmy had applied for a lease on a one-acre parcel at the lake and had been promised it, providing certain improvements were carried out. According to the Parks Branch, they entered an agreement that would have been turned into a ten-year lease had the improvements been done. But the improvements were not completed to their satisfaction and when Jimmy requested an extension they refused, offering instead a yearly permit for the cabin and boathouse that were in place, as an adjunct to the Bow Lake development. Jimmy provided a typical Simpson response to the Superintendent's letter:

I see that open season for fault finding is in the offing ... Past correspondence of mine asked for a renewal of a lease, not a permit, which is of no more use than a fifth wheel on a baby buggy. The late Commissioner of Dominion Parks, Mr. Harkin, considered the development then of sufficient value to grant such & since twice the sum is necessary for completion I cannot see why departmental action regarding another lease should be witheld. I would also request improvement of the trail from the highway to Hector Lake so that the expense of transporting building material does not run so much per square inch instead of per thousand feet.

This matter was still outstanding when the Bow Lake lease came up for review in 1942. The situation was exacerbated by Parks' intention to renew the Bow Lake rights by license of occupation for 21 years rather than by lease, which had a stronger legal standing. Jimmy expressed his concern about the apparent weakening of his tenure, but the officials replied that his original lease was an "odd parcel lease" issued in the twenties for lands outside of townsites and it was no longer available. Much of the fight had gone out of him since Margaret's death and, after being assured that his rights would not be affected, Jimmy continued to request a new lease but was resigned to the fact that he would have to accept the license of occupation. At the same time, in February, 1943, he informed the government that he wanted to keep the Hector Lake site and would accept a permit of occupation for it on a yearly basis. The new "License to Occupy a Chalet and Bungalow Campsite" at Bow Lake issued on March 12, 1943 incorporated a slightly enlarged area of 4.8 acres and included two new restrictive clauses. One stated that the lodge could only be used during the summer season from April 1st to October 31st as a chalet and bungalow camp, thereby eliminating the possibility of getting involved in the growing ski industry, and the other required that the license could not be transferred or assigned without the consent of the Minister.

With the matter of his rights at Bow Lake at least temporarily out of the way, Jimmy now had to face the 1943 season without the help of his son. Up until 1942 Jimmy jr. had contined to operate the pack train and to help at the lodge in the summers while continuing to play hockey in the winters. However, the war situation was worsening and since he was 21 years old, Jimmy jr. felt it was time to serve his country; he enlsited in the Airforce that fall. Despite the fact that this left him short on help, Jimmy could not resist when an opportunity to indulge his knowledge of wildlife and to get back in the saddle was presented to him by the government in the spring of 1943.

In 1940 James Smart was appointed Controller of the National Parks

Bureau and in December Jimmy sent him a hand-painted Christmas card congratulating him on his promotion. Jimmy, in fact, had seen Smart as a likely candidate for the top job in national parks and had befriended him some years before, recognizing, as he had with Harkin, that it was best to know the top dog personally. Smart appreciated Jimmy's annual gifts, and had them framed to hang in his home, and the two corresponded on a number of matters. In April, 1942, in an attempt to make some small contribution to the war effort, Jimmy wrote to Smart indicating his willingness to act as an Honorary Fire Warden voluntarily patrolling the Banff-Jasper Highway from Bow Lake to the Columbia Icefield. Smart thanked him for the offer and suggested he would pass the idea on to the Superintendent, but nothing came of it that year. When he brought the matter up again the following spring, Smart asked him to consider another job the Bureau was interested in pursuing, the continuing investigation of wildlife populations in Banff and Jasper parks begun two years previously. According to Jimmy's later account, the purpose of the investigation was to head off a movement by the Calgary Fish and Game Association to have the park thrown open for big game hunting on the premise that game populations were being wiped out by predators anyway. Smart offered payment of $150 per month for Jimmy's personal services, plus the cost of horses, equipment and food for the biologist accompanying him. Jimmy accepted, and struck out on a four month adventure that would mark his last major expedition in the Canadian Rockies.

The biologist assigned to the project was Dr. Ian McTaggart Cowan of the University of British Columbia, a man who would eventually to become one of Canada's foremost wildlife authorities. He and Jimmy got on well immediately, and McTaggart Cowan later stated he felt that the summer was the most interesting and enjoyable one he had ever spent in the field, and that Jimmy had told him he shared the opinion. Their investigations took them through the northern portions of Banff Park and the southern part of Jasper Park before they took a swing north around Mount Robson to the Smoky River. The main intention was to examine the bighorn sheep and goat populations of these regions, as parks personnel believed that large herds of sheep inhabited the area around the head of the Snake Indian River north of Jasper. Jimmy was sceptical and when he saw the range his suspicions were confirmed. He commented that "there was not even enough food for the gophers to stay overnight unless they packed a lunch." He believed that the major sheep populations in the park were to be found at the head of the Southesk River, an area he had viewed from the Brazeau River years before and had speculated would be good habitat. Their investigations proved Jimmy right as they found that the area was alive with sheep, particularly rams. One of these provided Jimmy with perhaps the most amusing incident of his hunting career:

I took Professor Cowan up to the gap in the range, passed two big bunches of sheep as I went up, saw a lone ram on the top of a hill, above timberline of course, sneaked up on him with Dr. Cowan behind me, and jumped on his back. He went out from under me like a cablegram going over to the old country for more money. Then I happened to look to my left and there was a bunch of 86 rams in one bunch.

According to McTaggart Cowan, this first and only "flying tackle of a bighorn sheep" presented an extremely humourous sight: "Jim looked at me with a mischievous look in his eye and then he catfooted up to this sheep and jumped on its back and grabbed it around the neck. The old fellow staggered to his feet and threw Jim to the ground all covered with sheep hair and then dashed off a few yards and turned around to look back to figure out what was going on." A few days later while they were resting on a beautiful mountain slope after spending the day in a rigorous climb to The Cairn on Cairn Pass, during which Jimmy had been "climbing like a mountain goat all day," the tired young biologist was surprised to hear Jimmy say, "Well, this is quite a place to have your 67th birthday."

Over the course of the trip, McTaggart Cowan had the opportunity to observe the way Jimmy handled the camp and the pack train, and he was impressed with the habits imparted by almost 50 years on the trail. Jimmy still chose to use a tepee for camping, being one of the few outfitters who had not switched entirely to tents, and the biologist appreciated that fact that it allowed for a warm and cheerful campfire to be lit in its interior every evening. Less appreciated was the fact that when they arrived at each campsite Jimmy would find that his tepee poles, carefully left from previous visits years before, had been cut into tent poles by subsequent users, necessitating the cutting of thirteen new poles at each stop amid much cussing and swearing.

McTaggart Cowan also marvelled at the way Jimmy treated the horses, and how he at several times put their welfare above the schedule of the party. He noted that Jimmy did not believe in shoeing his horses because with shoes on they could not feel the nature of the trail they were travelling. But in this case, since they were on a four month trip, he compromised and shod their front feet. Similarly, Jimmy didn't believe in hobbling his horses at night, as he felt it wasn't fair to them after they had been working all day. Although this meant he had to catch them each morning, he was willing to spend the extra time in what he felt was their best interests.

As the trip progressed, the two developed a very close relationship despite the difference in their ages. McTaggart Cowan reflected on this and came to the conclusion that it was because each man had something to offer the other. He found Jimmy "an extraordinary observant man who was an absolute goldmine of completely reliable information" gathered over a lifetime, able to recall when the bighorn had been abundant or scarce in different locales and all the factors that had influenced this. On the other hand, for Jimmy his biological knowledge provided "a framework under which he could fit all kinds of observations made over a long and very observant life so that it started to build up into a pattern that made sense."

That McTaggart Cowan had made a convert became apparent as Jimmy became progressively more interested in his biological studies. For example, McTaggart Cowan gathered wolf scats so that they could be examined to determine what the predators were eating in the area. This involved picking up the scats when they were discovered, noting information on when and where they were found, and then sealing them in special plastic bags carried in the biologist's saddle bags. McTaggart Cowan noted that Jimmy often preferred to walk ahead with his horse instead of riding, something he had done for much of his guiding career. On these occasions the biologist recalled that "I felt that it was almost my ultimate triumph as an educator when I found the wolf scats hanging from the low branch of a tree where I could pick them off without even getting off my horse." Soon after returning from this lengthy expedition in early September, Jimmy wrote to report to Smart and received a letter in return that laid out the possibility of continuing the work the following summer. He then departed to guide Jasper Park Superintendent James Woods up the Alexandra River and into the country around the Castleguard Meadows. When he returned, he received a copy of McTaggart Cowan's report for the summer, along with a request that he go over it, check out any details and make suggestions for changes. When the final report appeared, it paid him a high compliment:

Above all it is the writer's wish to express his sincere appreciation of the efforts of James Simpson, guide and outfitter for the expedition. His knowledge of the terrain, his interest in the game, enthusiasm for the study, and unfailing good humour contributed immeasurably, in ways that will be understood by those who have spent like periods in similar endeavours under the vicissitudes of montane conditions.

Although he had been looking forward to it, Jimmy was not able to take the government up on the offer to continue the work during the summer of 1944. He expressed his intention to do so right up until the beginning of the summer but then found that he could find absolutely no reliable men to take on work at the lodge. The previous summer had been hard on Billie because she had been left virtually alone to run the lodge while Jimmy was out on the trail and Mary was touring with "Ice Capades." Apart from serving the guests, she had the constant worry of keeping one jump ahead of the rationing officials, who periodically dropped in to check if wartime food rationing regulations were being complied with. She had worked out a routine for their visits whereby she would open a can of peas and show them that it was three-quarters water and one-quarter vegetables, and then claim that such supplies were not capable of feeding hungry people in the wilderness where appetites were large. Nevertheless, it was just one more strain on her and Jimmy realized that it could not continue.

Jimmy made arrangements to provide his outfit for McTaggart Cowan's study and he spent the summer working at the lodge. In the final analysis, he need hardly have bothered, for very few guests registered over the entire season. At $6.00 per guest per day he might well have been better off out on the trail doing the biological work. To make matters worse, he was involved in his first full-fledged accident that July after half a century of travel in the Rockies in all kinds of harrowing conditions. And, in an ironic twist of fate, it did not occur out in the wilderness but on the Banff-Jasper Highway. It happened when he was driving some important guests, New York opera critic Carlton Smith and his singer-wife Ginny, to view the Columbia Icefield. On the way home Jimmy was driving around a bend in the highway near Hilda Creek when a tire blew and he swerved across the road to avoid going over a steep bank. Unluckily, the car rolled on the shoulder of the road and as Jimmy was driving with his arm out the window it was crushed as the vehicle went over. The arm was horribly gashed as well as being broken and several weeks of healing were required before it could even be put in a cast. But despite the severity of the injury and his age, he recovered quickly, and accomplished most of his rehabilitation on the woodpile at the lodge.

If the war years were mainly a time of trial for the Simpsons, the post-war period was just the opposite. The tourist business turned around quickly and the trickle of tourists soon became a flood as more and more people in an increasingly affluent society turned to the automobile to see the country, as Jimmy had accurately predicted. At the end of the war Jimmy jr. played semi-professional hockey for two years, first with the Minneapolis Millers and then with the Vancouver Canucks. In the summer and fall, though, he handled the outfitting and virtually all the maintenance at the lodge. As mentioned, Jimmy had never been mechanically inclined, and in an age where mechanization was the key to efficiency he depended entirely on the mechanical skills that his son had picked up in technical school and the Airforce. These skills were added to constantly as Jimmy jr. worked with local plumbers, electricians and carpenters to gain the knowledge necessary to keep the lodge going. At the same time, the business of managing the lodge was becoming more onerous for Jimmy and Billie as they advanced in years. This was particularly true in light of the increasing number of guests wanting to use the rather limited facilities at Bow Lake, and in the face of this Mary took on an increasing share of the responsibility for guest services and reservations when she was not teaching in Omaha. The assistance of his family allowed Jimmy to concentrate on his dreams for expansion.

Even before he had finished the first part of the main lodge in 1940, Jimmy had recognized that accommodating 12 guests in the main building and a few more in the cabins was not going to suffice for the future. Early in the war years he had actually begun some work on foundations for an extension, but of course this work had to be curtailed before long. After the war, he set his sights on an addition that would incorporate at least 20 new guest rooms, as well as badly needed new kitchen and dining facilities to properly serve the needs of the increased number of guests. The problem he faced was the usual one —where to get the capital funds to do the work. This time it was his friends and neighbours Peter and Catharine Whyte who came to the rescue.

The Whyte family had had a long and close relationship with the Simpsons. Jimmy had bought most of his outfitting supplies from Peter's father Dave, one of the pioneer general merchants in town, and the families lived near each other on the Bow River. During the early years, when all the cooking at Bow Lake was done in a tent in front of the original cabin, Dave White felt badly at seeing Billie trying to cook over a fire on the ground, so he gave her a cook stove to work on as a gift. Peter Whyte and his wife Catharine, whom he had met at art school in Boston and had married in 1930, painted almost annually at Bow Lake and were treated like family during their sojourns there. As the couple had considerable funds at their disposal, with Catharine's family having a major interest in one of the United States' largest engineering firms, they were delighted to help out and agreed to lend money to Jimmy jr. and Mary to invest in the addition to the lodge.

In accordance with his usual practice, Jimmy began work on the addition in 1948, before the plans were submitted and approved. Ken Jones, who had worked as a packer and cook in the Rockies since 1930 and had learned the techniques of log building working with B. C. homesteaders and road cribbers, was hired to head the team of six or seven builders. As with the original lodge, the first job was to lay in a sufficient supply of building logs, and Jimmy jr. worked with Jones and his men to secure them at the Silverhorn Creek burn. However, one wall in the addition was to be just over 76 feet and for these logs the crew scoured the tall timber around Hector Lake. About thirty 80 foot plus green trees were cut in order to have a selection for the seven that were going to be needed for the building, and after just about killing several horses in an attempt to skid them out through the heavy forest a small caterpillar tractor was found to assist in the chore. With great difficulty the trees were loaded onto a truck with a bolster and hauled to Bow Lake, where they were trimmed and dry-decked so that the best and straightest would be ready for construction use the following spring.

Jimmy had asked Karl Hansen to prepare some preliminary plans for the extension in 1939 and, as mentioned, he had done some work on the foundations before the war. However, over the intervening years his ideas had changed somewhat and consequently he did not have a final plan down on paper. Therefore, when construction was set to start he took Jones down to the beach and drew out his plan — essentially a two storey, roughly 60 foot square structure designed to attach to the north side of the existing building. After committing the design to memory, Jones began laying out and building the stone foundation. Jimmy would go along and measure it out from memory and Jones' men would peg and string it off. Concrete footings were required to support the walls and all the cement had to be mixed in a wheelbarrow on the spot, using water and glacially-washed gravel hauled from the lake. Next came the stone foundation wall itself, again constructed of stone gathered near-by from rock blasted out during the construction of the highway. On top of this was placed the first round of logs, each one of them cut with a round notch to fit tightly over the next one, so that very little chinking was required. These logs were pegged down with drift pins every eight feet to prevent them from moving and fitted at the corners with a squaw notch. After all the preliminary work of taking out the logs and building the foundation was done, there were only about three weeks of building weather left in the fall of 1948 for log work. Building recommenced as soon as the weather allowed the next spring and it took them about three months to complete the basic shell of the lodge.

When questioned about his plans by park authorities in 1948, Jimmy gave the standard reply, "Mr. Walter Painter is preparing these but we must both be patient as Mr. Painter cannot sit at a drafting board for any length of time but will have them ready long before the time is ripe to get at such construction." In a desperate attempt to get something to approve, Park Superintendent James Hutchison asked Jimmy jr. on one occasion to see if he could stir his father up on the plans. When his son asked him if they could get something for parks, Jimmy replied, "Tell them its simple — it goes up like this, up like this and then up like this and then its got a roof on it." Another problem developed in early 1949 when the plans were finally ready, because Jimmy disagreed with some of the ideas that Painter had come up with, including making the addition three storeys high instead of two and building it entirely of log instead of one storey in log and the other in frame covered with log siding. Because the architect was a good friend, Jimmy did not want to fight with him over this. Fortunately the government officials, happy to have any plans at all, continued to allow him to build the way he wanted rather than strictly according to the plans. A building permit in the amount of $30,000 was finally issued in November, 1949.

Most of the work was carried out during the 1949 season, but it was apparent that it would not be finished in time for opening in 1950. Jimmy therefore decided to finish off the dining room, kitchen and ten guest rooms on the ground floor and to make them available for the season before finishing off the second storey when the guests had departed. This was also necessary because a redesign of the second floor was occasioned by a happy event. On October 6, 1949 Jimmy jr. married Lorna (Larri) Oliver, daughter of old friends Dave and Lorna Oliver and granddaughter of Frank Wellman, the outfitter to whom Jimmy had sold his interest in the Kootenay Plains ranch in 1918. The second storey was now to accommodate a large four-room suite that would be the newlyweds' year-round living quarters.

Despite not having the building completed as he had hoped, the move into it in July, 1950 was a memorable day in Jimmy's life. Catharine Whyte, who was present for the occasion, described it in a letter to her mother:

It was a full house, Miss Hinman and nine elderly ladies and a lot of other guests. Mary and Jimmy had it all pretty well planned. Big Jim had his first fire in the new tremendous dining room fireplace and all was set. In order to move the stove and refrigerator out they had to cut a large hole in the old kitchen wall, which the carpenters did, and then everyone started helping to move things. As soon as the guests saw the staff and the carpenters start carrying things they pitched in too and we were like a lot of ants going back and forth in a steady stream. . .   Dr. Wood seemed to be interested in kitchen things and I passed him with gloves on and hot stove lids, for they had to cook supper on the stove before it was moved. That too took about 10 men and came through the wall they had cut, through what will be the entrance hall, then the curio room and then the dining room and through the big door into the kitchen . . . Jimmy also had to move the sort of fountain thing where they get cold water for drinking in the dining room, and while we were setting up the tables for breakfast they were moving in lounge furniture so that when we went back into the living room part where the old dining room had been I was quite surprised to find it full of chairs and two sofas that Jimmy had gotten trucked up from their house in Banff. They had hung a couple of pictures in the afternoon and the electricians had even gotten the lights up.

It was really wonderful to see how everyone pitched in, including the cowboys, and really enjoyed it too. . . Big Jim was so pleased to see his dream coming true that he just stood and watched and every once in a while would let out a real laugh and slap someone on the back.

The good feeling that Catharine Whyte described had by that time become a hallmark of the operation of Num-Ti-Jah Lodge, as the spelling of the name had come to be in the post-war years to bring the pronunciation more into line with the way the old Stoneys would say it. Virtually everyone who visited felt it and many took the time to write the Simpsons and express their feelings. A typical example was a letter written by a young lady named Janet Williams from Illinois who visited during the same period as the move into the new lodge was going on. She enthused: "I have never been to a place where the people are so friendly and treat you as if you were actually a member of their family. That is what I liked most about Bow Lake. It has a warmness in it and the atmosphere is so friendly. When you come you get a hearty welcome and when you leave you get a friendly goodbye and are cordially asked to come again."

With new and enlarged facilities and such word-of-mouth testimonials, soon to be bolstered by the lodge's first promotional brochure, the vision that Jimmy and Billie had held for Num-Ti-Jah was soon achieved. But, as Jimmy wrote Dr. Thorington in 1952, "When I set out to build this new place I thought I would get more time to relax & ponder my past misdeeds but I find those thoughts were but a liquid dream." With the completed lodge and the four cabins now capable of accommodating up to 70 guests a night and the flow of tourists coming to the Rockies increasing every year, operating the facility became increasingly hectic. Serving the needs of the visitors now required the hiring of considerable summer staff in addition to the wranglers, who had been a part of the scene for several years, and problems of running a hotel in a remote location far from the source of services such as power and sewerage had to be creatively dealt with. Essentially it meant that the operating of the lodge had to be put on a modern footing, a fact recognized by the Simpson family members in 1952. Up to this point Jimmy had never legally incorporated his business, running it in the old fashioned way where a man's word and a handshake were all that was needed. But the times had changed and on August 18, 1952 Simpson's Num-Ti-Jah Lodge Ltd. was incorporated under the Companies Act of the Province of Alberta.

CHAPTER TWELVE

Tales of the Mountain Man

Throughout his life, Jimmy had always been a gregarious individual, capable of handling all kinds of people in many different situations. With the completion of the lodge and the incorporation of the business, the public relations abilities he had picked up while handling the vicissitudes of an outfitting and guiding business for half a century were to be utilized to the fullest. As the fifties progressed into the sixties and large numbers of tourists used the facilities, he was increasingly called on to greet and entertain them with the wit, humour and idiosyncratic behaviour expected of one who had pioneered the country. To a large degree, Jimmy enjoyed his reputation as a "mountain man" and happily performed the role that visitors had heard about and expected to see. Drawing from his vast store of experience in the mountains and freely embellishing the tale if the situation warranted it, he kept many a visitor entertained around an after-dinner fireplace. However, they were times when being the pioneer wore a little thin and he would avoid the public and concentrate on the never-ending work to be done on the lodge or on his hobbies of painting, reading, writing and stamp collecting.

Catharine Whyte was one of the first to make note of Jimmy's reputation in 1954 when a busload of people arrived at the lodge: "One lady got out & asked if Jim Simpson was here. He came out & it seems she was a niece or granddaughter or something of Sir William Van Horne. She was only here a few minutes. We were amused for when Jim appeared all the people on the other side of the bus stood up to see what Jim looked like as if he were a bear or something & he rose to the occasion and waved them off." To add to his reputation, Jimmy never varied his clothes or appearance, making them a trademark just as he had done as a young guide in the Rockies. He always wore an open-necked shirt, with a vest and an open jacket if necessary, but never a full-length coat no matter how cold the weather, and usually he had a pipe in his hand or clenched in his teeth. With his blue eyes and weather-beaten face topped off by the usual wide-brimmed Mounted Police hat, he was an impressive sight to the uninitiated.

Over the years Jimmy had built up a repertoire of stories and humourous repartee that he could use in different situations as they arose. For example, sometimes tourists were incredibly naive and, as Jimmy described to Dr. Thorington, he had to be prepared with a response no matter how preposterous the question:

This is my summer life these days:
    Que. Mr. Simpson, do you turn off the waterfall at the Glacier & turn it on again when the tourists are getting up in the morning?
    Ans. Yes, we have a big cork up there that connects with the machine that plugs the holes.
    Que. When did you come here?
    Ans. 1897. I saw the country grow up. In fact it was all prairie then.
    Que. What was it like?
    Ans. I was camped here alone when a peculiar looking canoe, something like a Venetian gondola came up the lake & a man in a light blue suit, something like velveteen, in it. When he beached the canoe I went down & said "To whom have I the pleasure of speaking this morning?" He doffed his hat & answered "I am Senor Christopher Columbus." To which a dear old lady listener said "It was eh?"
    And there was another this fall. A lady had been reading about Sir George Simpson, the explorer, so I got this:
    Que. Are you related to Simpson the explorer?
    Ans. Yes, in a corkscrew way. His family used to take in our family washing.

Sometimes, when he was trying to get some work done and was being pestered with questions, he took a more direct approach. Often he would move rocks around in his wheelbarrow, usually to fill in the holes in the access road or for repairs to the lodge. As Jimmy told it, on one occasion while he was doing some wheelbarrow work a woman approached him with, "What are you splitting those rocks for?" Without batting an eye he answered, "I'm doing time." "Are your really?" she replied aghast, "What was your crime?" "I murdered a woman," he deadpanned. "Whatever made you do such a thing?" she exclaimed. "She asked too many questions."

In a more serious vein, there were several stories that he would tell to interested guests, newspapermen or visiting friends about events that had really occurred at the lodge, usually featuring animals. One that was often heard after 1955 concerned the moose that broke his arm that year, the first and only time that he was seriously injured by an animal. It happened when he, Jimmy jr. and Larri were working on putting in a new bunkhouse at the corrals near the lodge on a July afternoon. A bull moose had been hanging around the area, which was quite a common occurrence, and so even though they knew he was nearby they paid no particular attention to him. Jimmy had just lifted a plank to move it out of the way when Jimmy jr., who was coming out of the packshack door, saw the moose charging out of the bush. He yelled at his father to look out, but Jimmy was becoming deaf in one ear and he just turned to his left to try to hear what Jimmy jr. was yelling. When he did turn to look to the right, he saw the moose just as it was upon him and he put up his right arm to protect himself as he rolled to avoid the charge. The moose kicked Jimmy's arm as it went by and broke it, so once more he had to go to Banff to have an arm put in a cast. Jimmy joked about the incident, quipping that "at least it wasn't my drinking arm," and "I've hunted them all my life, now they're hunting me."

Other animal stories concerned the exploits of goats around and about the lodge. The first related to the early days at Bow, about 1927, when he and two of his men were at the lake and saw an unusual sight, two goats swimming the lake. They went out in the boat to check out the phenomenon more closely and when they saw that the goats were having difficulty, they shepherded them towards the nearest shoreline. After they had helped them out of the water, the exhausted animals laid down to warm themselves on the beach, and Jimmy took out his camera to get a picture. As he dropped his eyes to line up the camera, one of the goats revived itself and started to charge him. When he saw the animal coming at him through the viewfinder, he instinctively stepped backwards into the water to avoid the charge, and fell over on his back for an ice cold dunking.

The other goat that made an impression at Num-Ti-Jah did so in the late 1950s. The season was over, the lodge empty and Jimmy was there alone while Jimmy jr. was in Banff with one of the men. While he was sitting out in the sun doing a sketch, his setter dog took after an old billy that had strayed down off the mountainside. Fearful that his dog would get hooked on the goat's horns, he tried to intervene, only to have the goat go tearing through the laundry building and then around the back of the lodge, followed by the dog in hot pursuit. Jimmy rushed after them, only to see the goat run smack into the door and then hop up on the windowsill and go crashing through the glass, carried by its momentum. Scared out of its wits, it ran across the room, jumped over the sofa and ran across a batch of watercolours Jimmy had laid out to dry, into a small lounge. There Jimmy cornered the animal. It dropped its ears down and tried to charge but it couldn't get any traction on the polished floor and fell on its head. Jimmy quickly dispatched it with a 22 calibre pistol, the only weapon available. The story continued:

Then I heard the gravel flying under spinning tires outside as some tourist who had heard the shooting decided he wasn't going to stay.

When Jim came in he was mad as the dickens because the man he had had with him had got awful tight. He came in and saw the broken windows and the mess and said "What's been going on?" Then he saw the goat in the lounge and said "You damn fool, you've been up on the mountain shooting goat." I said "No, no, not me" and pointed to the pile of goat excrement on the floor where it had voided its bowels in all the excitement. Jim looked at it and said, "Dad, I've got to believe you — you'd never pack that stuff down off the mountainside."

With his vast store of tales and reminiscences, always told to his friends and acquaintances with humour and a twinkle in his eye, it was not surprising that people pressed Jimmy to write his stories down for posterity. Dr. Thorington, as a student and writer of mountain history, was the most persistent and after assisting him with information and rememberances on their mutual friend the Austrian climbing guide Conrad Kain for a biography that Thorington published in 1935, Jimmy agreed to give it a try when he could find the time:

As to the book; well some time. What I have in mind is one entitled "Before the Road went through" dealing with the country which will be the Louise-Jasper Highway. The old time material, incidental, actual, & historical is legion. The historical part will take a lot of research unless I can get collaboration from such as yourself who has it at his fingertips. Backed with color plates it ought to make a real entertaining compilation of reading.

The incidental part of it dealing with such things as the old time guides' doings, such as Lusk, Peyto, Stephens, Vavasour, Peacock, Ballard & others would, if it can be depicted properly, make a story which is amusing & historical, each incident dealing with or connecting with a part of the landscape under immediate discussion such as Wilcox Pass, Waterfowl, Pyramid Peak & the upper falls of the north fork, etc. etc. Some of this material would flatly contradict the generally acknowledged later period historical data, but what of it?

The idea of a book remained in his mind for another ten years before he began to give it active consideration again, this time in response to a prompting by the noted editor of *Maclean's Magazine*, Scott Young. In reply, Jimmy stated he wasn't sure whether it was a shortage "of energy or pale ale" that was responsible for his indecision about writing some of his reminiscences down. But he did agree to write a piece for the magazine, tentatively called "Reminiscences of a Guide," which would allow him literary license to put together a story that was a composite of many of his experiences with clients on the trail. The story appeared under the title "My Prize Dude" in the June 15, 1946 edition of *Maclean's*, and its subject was a one month hunting trip with the Hon. George Percival Anthony Choldmeley of Keswich Manor, England, or "Clarence" for short. During the outing everything that could go wrong for a guide did go wrong, including having the guest break into a rousing chorus of "John Peel" whenever game was spotted and ending with him shooting his horse when he mistook it for a moose.

As time went on, Jimmy found the idea of writing freewheeling pieces such as "My Prize Dude" based loosely on the characters he had known to be more appealing than the more constraining idea of a book. The perils of writing a book were brought home to him with the appearance of two volumes of reminiscences by fellow guides, *The Trail to the Charmed Land* by Ralph Edwards in 1950 and *I Would Do It Again* by Bob Campbell in 1959, in which he found both authors prone to exaggerate the events in which they had taken part. Likewise when his old boss Tom Wilson's stories appeared as a serial in the local newspaper Jimmy accused him of being full of hot air in his claims to exploits as an outfitter and guide. Thus, he recognized that if he wrote and published his own story, he too would be a target for those who disagreed with his particular interpretation of events. Therefore, while never totally dismissing the idea of the book, he continued to write magazine stories, mainly for smaller western publications. Instead, the ideas for the book that he had put together in his mind became the material for interviews with newspaper journalists, writers, radio broadcasters, television producers, film-makers and, not least of all, historical researchers, who flocked to question him about the history of the Canadian Rockies and his part in it. In fact, it was his old friends Peter and Catharine Whyte who about 1950 acquired one of the first tape recording machines produced and did an interview with Jimmy in 1952 that would be saved in their museum, the Whyte Museum of the Canadian Rockies, for posterity.

While much of Jimmy's time at the lodge was spent telling and occasionally writing stories, his favourite pastime was going off alone to sketch and paint. As he got older, his family used to worry sometimes about where he was, but he never went too far and he could still take care of himself. Most of his paintings were done as Christmas cards or gifts for his friends, as Jimmy didn't believe that they were saleable, but Billie's Scottish upbringing made her feel that they had some value. After the war, Num-Ti-Jah had a small gift and curio shop that she and Mary ran and after Jimmy had painted enough to decorate the new rooms he began producing a few for sale in the shop. They became a big hit with the visitors to the lodge, and soon people were writing to order a watercolour landscape done personally for them. Jimmy happily obliged and soon found that he needed to paint summer and winter to keep up with the demand. He discovered that he enjoyed painting the winter scenes in summer and the summer scenes in winter. He also provided advice to the numerous amateur painters who came to paint the lake, surprising them with the depth of understanding of art and its techniques he had achieved over the years. When they saw the walls of the lodge adorned with his collection and heard the story attached to each one, they understood.

As time went on, Jimmy became more concerned about his art collection, as much of it had become irreplaceable and very valuable. Because he was afraid to leave it at the lodge over the winter, he would load it in the back of the pickup truck over the protests of Jimmy jr. and haul it back to Banff to put up in the house. In the spring, the same procedure would happen in reverse, until eventually he recognized that something had to be done. He was particularly concerned about his Rungius paintings, and as he and the artist were still the best of friends, sharing their August birthdays together either at Rungius' studio-home or the lodge, he talked with him about their ultimate disposition. Jimmy believed that there should be some lasting memorial to Rungius in Banff and he took it upon himself to bring the subject up with government officials, indicating that he would be happy to donate his collecton if such a thing could be arranged. Although some plans were discussed for the government museum, nothing positive could be worked out and Jimmy wasn't about to give his paintings up without some ironclad guarantees; he was concerned that otherwise they might find their way into the office of some politician in Ottawa. He found a solution through an acquaintance he made with Eric Harvie, a Calgary lawyer, oil magnate and philanthropist.

In the 1950s Harvie began to amass a collection of art, artifacts and other historic materials under the aegis of his Glenbow Foundation, which would form the basis of Calgary's Glenbow Museum. Harvie was particularly interested in western art and artists at this time and had set his sights on acquiring as much Rungius material as he could. By 1954 he had convinced Rungius to sell him his home and collection in Banff so that they could be preserved for posterity, and early in 1958, after Rungius had decided that he was too old to return to the Rockies, Harvie began negotiations to acquire the substantial contents of his studio in New York.

Jimmy continued to correspond with his old friend after his last visit to Banff in 1957 and he was aware that these negotiations were taking place. His belief in Carl's importance and the need for some recognition had not diminished. In fact, he had agreed to loan his eight Rungius pieces along with 16 other works from his collection for an exhibition at the Banff School of Fine Arts during the summer of Rungius' last visit. From there, at Harvie's request, he agreed that they could go on to an exhibition at the Calagary Allied Arts Centre and then to the Foundation's offices during the fall of 1957. The pieces were returned to Jimmy in November, but having seen them Harvie began to try to convince Jimmy to sell so that they could be joined with Carl's own material and other major western art collections that he was acquiring. In the spring of 1958 Jimmy agreed to loan eight Rungius, two Fuertes, one Goodwin, one Groll, two Russells, and nine Thorburns to Harvie for safekeeping while negotiations continued. Although he was interested in his collection's preservation, Jimmy had been a hard bargainer all his life and he intended to remain so, and he asked prices for much of the material that were in excess of what the knowledgeable Harvie thought they were worth. The discussions dragged on and finally, in the summer of 1959 just a few months before Rungius' death in October, an agreement was reached and Jimmy received $15,800 for the 23 pieces that had been on loan. Meanwhile, in 1958 he had been forced to admit to himself that his own paintings were worthy of being called "art" when Harvie's Glenbow Foundation bought one of his pieces to be included in its permanent collection of Alberta artists.

Apart from painting and writing, much of Jimmy's leisure time was spent with Billie, reading and writing letters in the evenings. During the summer they lived in the original octagonal cabin, or "Ram Pasture" as it came to be known, and there they could escape the press of tourists and guests if they wished. In the winter they would return to the house in Banff while the lodge was closed up and would spend much of their time visiting friends. Jimmy's fondness for the bottle and a good game of cards had not abated over the years and during the quiet winter months he found lots of opportunity to spend time with those of his cronies who felt likewise. However, early each morning he could be found in his friend Gus Baracos' Banff Cafe shooting the breeze or talking over the issues of the day with the proprietor and his other close friend Father Robert McGuinness, the Catholic priest.

Many of the Simpsons' wide circle of friends, aware of the couple's love of books, would send copies of material they found that they knew would interest them — botany for Billie and exploration literature for Jimmy. These they would read while listening to the news of the day on the radio, as both of them were particularly interested in world politics. In November, 1952 Billie expressed her pleasure at the election of President Eisenhower in the United States, noting in a letter to a friend that in her opinion "there was always such nice people visited the west when the last Republican Government was in, in the U.S.A." In the same letter she enthused on the christening of their first grandson, David Justin, who had been born to Jimmy jr. and Larri, and reported that "Jim Sr. dressed up for the occasion and really behaved in Church."

As the fifties progressed, many improvements were made at Num-Ti-Jah as Jimmy jr. took charge. In 1953 a powerhouse to hold a diesel generator for electricity was built, in 1954 staff quarters were constructed from the remnants of the Mountainholm Lodge in Banff and the same year the lodge received its first steam heating. A new license of occupation was offered by the government in 1954, including an additional area of 1.12 acres to incorporate the water supply and corral area, and in 1955 Jimmy accepted it. This allowed for the construction of a new bunkhouse for the trail hands who worked for Jimmy jr. in his outfitting business, which continued to be a successful operation, particularly for the fall hunting business, in conjunction with the pony business at the lodge. Occasionally Jimmy would accompany his son with the horses, but after one last ten-day outing to the Freshfields in 1953 with the William O. Field family, he rode no more. Interestingly, Billie, who had never really had the opportunity to go out much with Jimmy during his active days, now went out with her son on an occasional trip and marvelled at the beauty of the mountain flowers and mountain fastnesses that she had largely missed during earlier years.

Because of changing circumstances in the the Simpson family, the lodge business underwent a change in 1957 with the departure of Mary Simpson. She had continued to teach skating at Omaha in the winter and to work at the lodge in the summer until she retired from skating in 1955 and came back to Bow Lake to live. That same year Jimmy jr. and Larri had a second son, Gordon, and it soon became apparent that income from the lodge would not be sufficient to support the entire growing Simpson family. A decision was made to leave the future of the family's business in Jimmy jr.'s hands and Mary returned to the United States, but she soon moved to Flin Flon, Manitoba where she married Russ Hallock. After a few years there the Hallocks moved to Ft. St. James, B.C. with their daughter Cathy and established a very successful machine shop business, "Fort Machine Works."

Mary, as Jimmy described her, was "a real live wire" and her leaving was a sad time for he and Billie, but they kept in close contact by letter and later she was able to visit them fairly frequently. They were consoled by the pleasure afforded them by being able to watch their grandsons grow up and by the many friends and interesting visitors who continued to frequent the lodge. Num-Ti-Jah had always been a favourite spot for those who had met Jimmy or been out with him during his trail days, as they took the opportunity for a pleasant stay in one of their old camping spots and a chance to chew over "the good old days." Dr. Thorington and his wife came often, as did the Browne family and the Alfred Castle family. Other noteworthy visitors who occasionally appeared in the guest register were actors Robert Cummings and Burl Ives, writer Dale Carnegie, climber and British politician Colonel Leopold Amery and hockey broadcaster Foster Hewitt.

Meanwhile, changes were afoot at Num-Ti-Jah with respect to its seasonal operation. By the mid-fifties the Banff-Jasper Highway was being ploughed in the winter, and at one time James Smart had promised Jimmy that if and when this occurred the winter season restriction on the lodge would be lifted. About 1958 the lodge was broken into when it was closed up for the season and Jimmy jr. soon had his father convinced it was time to consider a year-round operation. They had to fully winterize and insulate the lodge and construct a new power plant, work that took several years for Jimmy jr. to complete, and it was not until 1962-

63 that the Simpsons launched their first winter season. To support the business, Jimmy jr. applied to put in a seasonal ski lift at Peyto Lake in 1964, but after the Simpsons had received the government's consent and made a substantial investment, the authorities changed their mind. Snowmobiling was suggested as an alternative and it became the mainstay of Num-Ti-Jah's winter business for the next 20 years.

As the fifties turned to the sixties, both Jimmy and Billie began to slow down considerably and to suffer the ailments that bother most people as they age. Billie had been afflicted with arthritis and she was also becoming very deaf. In 1961 Jimmy suffered a fall and broke a rib in his right side, and even he had to admit that he now moved a little slower. But his mind was just as active as ever, even if his body could not always follow suit. Jimmy jr., whose outfitting and guiding business continued to do well, indicated that he did not even have to advertise his business as Jimmy was advertising enough, both through his conversations with visitors and his frequent appearances in magazine and newpaper articles.

One of these, which appeared in the Toronto *Globe and Mail* in February, 1961 was entitled "His Name Is a Byword in the Rockies" and in it Jimmy threw down the gauntlet to the younger generation, which he described as "soft" and "so flabby they can't even walk to the end of the lake to fish." This became one of his common themes in his later years, but to those who did indicate they wished to meet some of the challenges he himself had faced in the mountains, he was a fount of information. As the *Globe and Mail* article concluded:

Today, Jimmy Simpson enjoys a life many might envy. In winter, he lives in Banff. In summer, when he feels in the mood, he packs up and takes a little jaunt through the mountains; or he works around the family lodge at Bow Lake. Only those who meet his exacting standards are priveleged to share briefly the exciting days of long ago when a man had to be a man to stay alive .

CHAPTER THIRTEEN

The Ram Pasture

Jimmy stood on the front porch of the new library and archives building constructed by his friend Catharine Whyte on the land adjacent to his home on Bear Street in Banff. It was Sunday, June 16, 1968 and beside him was his friend cowboy artist Charlie Beil, behind him was a group of admiring special guests, including Catharine Whyte and Billie, and in front of him was a crowd of some 500 people who had come to witness the opening of this important building for the preservation of Canadian Rockies history and culture. The Wa-Che-Yo-Cha-Pa Foundation (later Whyte Museum of the Canadian Rockies) had been built to honour the memory of the Banff pioneers, and at 91 and a resident for over 70 years Jimmy was pleased to accept Mrs. Whyte's invitation to represent them.

After Charlie Beil's remarks as guest speaker, Jimmy was called upon to perform the official opening ceremonies. As the press later reported it, he entertained the crowd with his "sparkling wit and wisdom" and then advised all the young people present to make good use of the contents of the building: "All men are born equal, but there is a chance for you in this great building of learning to improve yourselves." Having been a great reader and collector all his life, he spoke the words believing them implicitly. Then, he drew his razor-sharp hunting knife from its sheath and cut the buckskin thong across the entranceway while saying, "In the name of this gracious lady, Mrs. Catharine Whyte, who has donated this institution to the Banff people and the general public, I cut this ribbon and declare this building open."

The rest of the afternoon was spent in endless chinwags with friends and acquaintances from over the years who were among the crowd of 1,000 who thronged into the new facility that day. Jimmy was truly touched by this event, recognizing in it the fact that he had become part of the fabric of Canadian Rockies history. In a letter to a friend the following year, he indicated that he too was making a contribution to the future of the building, stating that in return for Catharine Whyte's help to him "I passed on my own building & lot for the future plans of a museum extension." In addition, he made arrangements that would ensure that some of his remaining artworks and part of his multitudinous collection of historic papers and photographs would be left to be preserved in the archives for posterity.

Having taken some steps that would guarantee him a little piece of immortality, Jimmy was soon reminded of his mortality. Although at 77 she was considerably younger than he, Billie's health had been failing for some time and shortly after the excitement of the opening she became seriously ill. She died on September 2, 1968 in the Banff Mineral Springs Hospital and, as was her wish, was cremated. Jimmy took her ashes to Bow Lake and kept them in the Ram Pasture over the winter until he could spread them in the spring in the secret, beautiful spot "where she said she would like to stay." His grief was tempered by the happy memories of the half century they had spent together, but he admitted to a friend that he hadn't realized how much he had depended on her and wrote another that "since the good lady passed on I have difficulty concentrating on any one subject, even watercolors."

Shortly after Billie's death, Jimmy received a letter from his old friend Dr. Thorington, with whom he had lost contact for some years. In answer to his question of how was he doing, Jimmy replied:

Am still going strong if not so fast as before, but old Father Time plays no favorites & I guess I cannot grumble as I have had my best days & no regrets.

Have not heard of any mountaineers worth that name for some years. Have not packed a horse or gone on the trail as nobody wants to do other than ride in a car, drink champagne out of plastic cups, then boast about roughing it to all and sundry. If you talk about the Freshfield or Castleguard they think it is something to eat, or going down the Saskatchewan Glacier on a saddle horse they ask, "When was that?" Your photograph in lodge of that event makes them shiver. Never-the-

less I have a good time every summer enlightening them that there were
people before their time who did things like that, so they ask "But why?"

Thorington wrote again shortly afterward and, as was his custom, was
full of questions concerning "the good old days" and some of the historic
characters of the Rockies Jimmy had known. While previously he had
found little time or patience to answer such queries in detail, Jimmy now
found that Thorington's questions were "like a new kind of pill for what
ails one" and he invited his friend to continue asking them. Thus began
a series of 38 letters, written between October, 1968 and February, 1972,
in which Jimmy laid out in a witty and sparkling fashion, undulled by his
ninety-odd years, the story of his life. In many ways, these letters
became the biography he had never written, and they have been liberally
borrowed from for the writing of this book. As well, he continued to
write some of his reminiscences in article form for the popular western
periodical *Golden West*. The last of these, "Peyto . . . of Peyto Lake,"
appeared in 1972 and fittingly dealt with tales of Bill Peyto, the man who
had inspired Jimmy to a lifetime of outfitting and guiding in the
Canadian Rockies and the one who he regarded as the foremost of the
Canadian mountain men.

Jimmy's generosity in sharing his memories with Thorington in
writing was duplicated in other ways. With television firmly ensconced
as the media in most favour with the general public, television producers
were constantly looking for a good story and it was inevitable that
sooner or later Jimmy would come to their attention. Having a vivid
memory of the days before radio, when the only transmissions were
those of orchestras in the heavens he heard when out on his trapline,
Jimmy was not overly enamoured with television but would watch it
occasionally. However, he was a born actor and could not resist giving
the producers what they wanted. The Calgary station CFCN did a
special programme in Banff featuring Jimmy and his bosom friend from
the Banff Cafe, Gus Baracos, the results of which were gleefully
reported in the *Crag and Canyon* newspaper:

One of the most exciting new TV comedy teams to appear in years made
its debut on the magic tube in Banff last week.

Gus Baracos, the astute Athenian, and Jimmy Simpson, whose theory is to always leave 'em laughing, upstaged everybody on the CFCN "Today in Banff" special programme at the Voyager Inn last week.

The jovial pair, who between them have almost spanned the history of Banff, drew rave notices from the program directors for their scintillating impromptu performance.

In flowing poetic terms Mr. Baracos discussed his impressions of the beauty of Banff, deftly played his mandolin, and interjected friendly barbs, which inspired his longtime friend Mr. Simpson to greater repartee.

Mr. Simpson's remarks about his association with Christopher Columbus and his interpretation of some parts of the Old Testament will long be remembered as some of the boldest wit ever telecast.

This broadcast was followed by a programme produced by the BBC on one of its more interesting expatriate sons. Jimmy cooperated fully in its making, entertaining the British film crew at Bow Lake, and answering the inevitable questions as to why he had never gone back. But he was not particularly happy with the result, and indicated that had he known what the producer was attempting to do "I would have added a bit more spice" and summing up his review with "frankly, I thought what I heard on repeat was punk."

Radio discovered Jimmy about the same time as television. The CBC was presenting a weekly hour-long programme called "Between Ourselves" at this time and in the spring of 1969 producer Fred Diehl approached Jimmy about being the subject of a segment of the series. He agreed and so began the most extensive and intensive series of interviews about his life that Jimmy would ever undergo. Diehl's approach and personality seemed to agree with him and Jimmy was completely at ease and candid in the approximately 11 hours of interviews he provided. Again his famous wit and love of storytelling shone through in these interviews, as a few excerpts illustrate.

On his friendship with legendary Calgary newspaperman Bob Edwards: "He came to Banff and asked my advice whether or not he should give up his newspaper and run for a seat in the Legislature. That way, he said, he could petition to have a pipeline run directly from the bar to his office. It was a pity that he died so young. Instead of burying him they should have poured him back into the barrel."

On the fear of heights: "I could look over a 400 foot drop with no problem. I once had a doctor out with me who said, "You know, I can't look over a cliff or I want to jump over." I said, "For God's sake don't, you haven't paid your bill yet."

On the parks department: "The government always gave me a bad reputation. I don't know why, possibly it was because I was the best poacher in Banff National Park. But whenever the government wanted something important done in the outdoors, it was me they picked on to do it."

On opera singer Enrico Caruso: "Otto Kahn was the chairman of the Metropolitan Opera and whenever we were in New York he gave me his box. I heard Caruso in Rigoletto. My God, you talk about melody. When Caruso wanted to he could set the opera back on its heels. It rolled out of him just like Scotch rolled down a drunk's throat."

On inspirational writer Dale Carnegie: "Dale Carnegie was staying here at the lodge writing his book . He said to me, ' Jimmy, how do you conquer fear?' I said, 'I don't know Dale, what's the feeling like?' "

On his hero Bill Peyto: "Old Bill Peyto had a finger bent over from the war. He went to the doctor and said, 'I want that thing cut off.' 'Alright, I'll give you an anaesthetic first,' said the doctor. 'The hell you will,' replied Peyto, I want to watch you do it so I can do it myself if it happens again.' "

The extensive series of interviews with Jimmy himself were supplemented with interviews from those who knew him in the heyday of his career, including Alfred Castle, Ken Jones, Mrs. Katherine Wedgwood, Dr. Ian McTaggart Cowan, and Foster Hewitt. These were moulded into a fascinating programme entitled "Nashan-esen," which was broadcast nationally on April 3, 1969. Many of Jimmy's friends heard it and took the time to write and tell him how the programme had enthralled them, and to compliment him on his never-failing zest for life.

Despite the fact that he sounded like a man 30 years his junior on the programme, the ravages of time were catching up with Jimmy. In the spring of 1967 he had become careless while working around the lodge in the bright sunshine and suffered a bad case of snowblindness. He took little notice of it at the time, having suffered it several times before in his career, but on this occasion he aggravated it by washing with a soap that had too much lye in it. This left one eye permanently red and weepy. He also admitted that his hearing was not as good as it had been, although he joked that "it's good enough I can still hear a 25 cent piece jingle in a sack of feathers."

Jimmy accepted these aggravations of advancing years philosophically and they did not lead him to mend his ways. He would still go out in -50 degree weather without a coat, as he had done all his life. Although his drinking had decreased as his years advanced, he still indulged and even overindulged occasionally. In December, 1968 he wrote to Doctor Thorington that he had celebrated some friends' anniversary at the lodge and reported "I took too much wine, got up in the morning with a taste in my mouth like the bottom of a parrot cage & said the usual, 'Never again!' "

Having decided not to go back to the house in Banff and to finish out his days in the Ram Pasture after Billie's death, Jimmy also continued to work hard at the lodge. He complained that "this tourist business minus the horse wears one's feet right down to the quick" and that "we are horribly busy, which is what I built the place for of course." The matter of Num-Ti-Jah's future had come to a head beginning in 1967 when the National and Historic Parks Branch, through Park Superintendent D. J. Learmonth, had made Jimmy jr. an offer of $76,000 to buy all the Simpson family's rights and improvements at Bow Lake. They discussed the matter and decided that the offer was not enough, but agreed to continue the negotiations. These resulted in an April, 1968 proposal that if the Simpsons were not interested in selling they could continue to operate much as they had in the past with a new lease. Discussions continued until February, 1969, at which time the Parks Branch upped its offer to $83,000 and a five year concession agreement to run the lodge and its ancilliary operations. Fiercely proud and independent, Jimmy, Jimmy jr. and Mary decided not to sell and to take the long-sought lease that had been offered.

The matter of the lease for Num-Ti-Jah settled, Jimmy could enjoy his last few years with peace of mind. During those years he continued to slow down, but he still tried to keep up with his correspondence and friendships when he could. In September, 1971 Catharine Whyte asked him to participate in a movie that her nephew Jon Whyte was doing with Filmwest Productions of Edmonton to fulfill his requirements for a Master's Degree in Communications at Stanford University. Jimmy somewhat reluctantly agreed, but once the cameras were set up and rolling and Mrs. Whyte began to ask him questions about his life the old stories came flooding back, even though he was a little vague on the dates. It was the last, and perhaps the most important, interview he ever gave, for when it appeared under the title "Jimmy Simpson, Mountain Man" it provided both a fine visual and oral record of the man and his life for future generations to enjoy. Unfortunately, Jimmy never lived to see it.

When asked about God and the hereafter, Jimmy had always claimed that he wasn't sure whether there was a God or not, and that people could only follow the ten commandments and hope there was. For him, if there was a God it wasn't the one of conventional religions, for which he never had much use. Rather, it was one that was a part of his mountains: "There is something up in the mountains, something that is far ahead of human beings and will always be far ahead of human beings. You don't know what it is and you don't know if it will be there after you die." As for the hereafter, he didn't personally believe there was one, feeling that when people died they would just drop off like the animals. Since he held such views, it was not surprising that he would constantly joke about his demise with his friends. In a letter to Dr. Thorington he wrote, "If the old boys have passed on to the place the good book says they should have, I am certain there is enough of them to have kicked Satan out & taken over the proprietorship themselves; if so we'll get a welcome." Even in the "Mountain Man" film he summed up: "I've had a very fine life. I wouldn't care if I knew death was coming at noon today, I could laugh right up till I was having a cup of soup."

The "fine life" came to an end on October 30, 1972 when Jimmy crossed his last divide, dying quietly in the Banff Mineral Springs Hospital. A few days later, on November 3rd, a funeral service was held in the Banff Funeral Home and, as was his wish, he was cremated. Tributes flowed into Jimmy jr. and Mary from all over North America. Even Prime Minister Pierre Elliott Trudeau sent a telegram which stated: "Jim Simpson was one of the great figures in the Rocky Mountain area in this century. His adventures and accomplishments as an explorer, trail blazer, botanist and guide will long be remembered by Canadians."

But the most lasting tribute to Jimmy was not to come until almost two years later. On August 8, 1974, the anniversary of what would have been his ninety-seventh birthday, his old adversary, now known as Parks Canada, held a dedication ceremony at Bow Lake to name a 9,700 foot peak that could be seen to the north-west of the lodge. Jimmy jr. and Mary unveiled a plaque that officially named Mount Jimmy Simpson to "pay tribute to this great individual whose life has portrayed the spirit of the Canadian Rockies." The mountain stands as a fitting memorial to Nashan-esen, legend of the Rockies, the last and greatest of the Canadian mountain men.

A NOTE ON SOURCES

For one with an academic training such as mine, the urge to use footnotes to source original material is a strong one. However, for this story, I resisted the urge. Somehow, to clutter up Jimmy's story with endless recitations of where the material came from seemed inappropriate. Therefore, I have chosen to provide information on where the material on Jimmy used in this story may be found in the form of this "Note."

Generally speaking, most of the material used in this work resides in the archives of my employer, the Whyte Museum of the Canadian Rockies. Much of Jimmy's correspondence and personal papers were generously donated to the archives by the Simpson family, Jimmy jr. and Mary Hallock, for my use in writing this story. This joined other of Jimmy's papers that had originally been given to Catharine Whyte by him before his death and then subsequently by the family over the years afterwards. It now resides in its totality in the archives and provides the best source of material originating from those whom Jimmy was in contact with. However, there is very little of Jimmy's own correspondence to them in this collection, or, indeed, anywhere else. It does contain some important exceptions — Jimmy's writings to Billie during the period of their courtship and immediately after their marriage and copies of all the manuscripts he wrote over the years.

The best sources of Jimmy's own correspondence lie in two other collections. One is the oft-quoted J. Monroe Thorington Collection in the Princeton University Archives (copies available at the Whyte Museum) which contains a series of thirty-eight letters written to Dr. Thorington by Jimmy, mainly in the nineteen-sixties, in which he related the story of his life in answer to the Dr.'s queries. A second is a collection of correspondence in the National Archives of Canada, National Parks Collection (RG 85) which detail his ups and downs with the federal government on several matters, but most particularly with respect to Bow Lake and Num-Ti-Jah Lodge. There are also several other collections at the Whyte Museum, in particular the Catharine Whyte papers, which contain correspondence and/or information on Jimmy and his activities over the years.

Perhaps the most enjoyable sources of material are those provided by Jimmy himself on the numerous tape recorded interviews in the Whyte Museum's collections. Beginning with Peter and Catharine's early tape with him in the 1950s, Jimmy was recorded on a more-or-less regular basis right up until his death. These include several tapes done over the years by archives employees and especially the work tapes done by CBC broadcaster Fred Diehl for the 1969 program "Nashan-esen."

And finally there were the reminiscences and anecdotes provided by Jimmy's family and friends, who never failed to provide those sparkling stories and fascinating bits of information that helped to tie this story together. I would like to thank all of those who provided their reminiscences so freely, but most especially to Mary Hallock and Jimmy jr. without whom the writing of this book would not have been possible.

INDEX